Space Policy Reconsidered

Published in Cooperation with
the Center for Space and Geosciences Policy,
University of Colorado, Boulder

Space Policy Reconsidered

EDITED BY

Radford Byerly, Jr.

Westview Press
BOULDER, SAN FRANCISCO, & LONDON

Westview Special Studies in Science, Technology, and Public Policy

This Westview softcover edition is printed on acid-free paper and bound in library-quality, coated covers that carry the highest rating of the National Association of State Textbook Administrators, in consultation with the Association of American Publishers and the Book Manufacturers' Institute.

Copyright © 1989 by University of Colorado, Boulder

Published in 1989 in the United States of America by Westview Press, Inc., 5500 Central Avenue, Boulder, Colorado 80301, and in the United Kingdom by Westview Press, Inc., 13 Brunswick Centre, London WC1N 1AF, England

Library of Congress Cataloging-in-Publication Data
Space policy reconsidered / edited by Radford Byerly, Jr.
    p.   cm. — (Westview special studies in science, technology, and public policy)
    Includes index.
    ISBN 0-8133-7819-2
    1. Astronautics and state—United States.   I. Byerly, Radford.
II. Series.
TL789.8.U5S59   1989
333.9′4′0973—dc 20   89-14633
                                                                                  CIP

Printed and bound in the United States of America

⊚   The paper used in this publication meets the requirements of the American National Standard
    for Permanence of Paper for Printed Library Materials Z39.48-1984.

10   9   8   7   6   5   4   3   2

WHERE THERE IS NO VISION, THE PEOPLE PERISH...

PROVERBS 29:18

WHERE NO COUNSEL IS, THE PEOPLE FALL; BUT IN THE MULTITUDE OF COUNSELLORS THERE IS SAFETY.

PROVERBS 11:14

Contents

Preface

For some time space policy debate has been too constrained by preexisting assumptions and programs: A need exists for open discussion to question those assumptions and critique those programs. There is also a related need for a community of independent space policy analysts in order to inform those discussions. The aim of this book is to take a step toward meeting such needs.

Accordingly, eleven essays have been solicited from thoughtful and involved space policy participants. Collectively they address most space policy issues, as input to discussion and debate.

The Introduction makes a case for independent policy analysis in terms of a needed paradigm shift and synthesis. The remaining chapters are grouped into four parts.

Part One provides three different overviews of the U.S. civilian space program from budgetary, historical, and managerial perspectives. With this context established, Part Two discusses policy issues in four chapters, each focused on a program activity area: transportation, science, applications, and infrastructure.

The two chapters of Part Three address the lack of economic and commercial philosophy in our space program, and the problems arising from that lack.

Finally, in Part Four two concluding overview essays show how perspectives from other disciplines can illuminate space policy issues and analysis, and point out future directions for research.

Where the book is successful, credit belongs principally to the chapter authors; where it is not, responsibility falls on me. In addition to the authors, several others have contributed, and two in particular should be mentioned: S. Alan Stern, who provided many useful comments, and Darlene Jeune, who produced the text. I thank all my helpers, some of whom did not care to be named.

Finally, the support of the Alfred P. Sloan Foundation and the University of Colorado is gratefully acknowledged.

Radford Byerly, Jr.
Boulder, Colorado, 1989

Contributors

Garry D. Brewer is Frederick K. Weyerhaeuser professor at Yale with appointments in the Schools of Organization & Management and Forestry & Environmental Studies. His research interests span several policy areas from war games to oceans.

Ronald D. Brunner is a professor of Political Science at the University of Colorado, and has been director of the Center for Public Policy Research. Currently studying the Space Station, he has previously worked on energy and social welfare policy.

Radford Byerly, Jr., is director of the Center for Space and Geosciences Policy at the University of Colorado. His policy experience includes several years on the staff of the House of Representatives Subcommittee on Space Science and Applications overseeing civil space programs.

Richard DalBello has directed several space-related projects at the Office of Technology Assessment, most recently a study of "Launch Options for the Future." He is currently with the Office of Commercial Space Programs, Department of Commerce.

Riccardo Giacconi, an X-ray astronomer, is director of the Space Telescope Science Institute at Johns Hopkins University. He has served on many scientific committees concerned with space science programs and policies.

Molly K. Macauley, an economist at Resources for the Future, directs a research program on space economics. She has written on the economics of space transportation and of the geostationary orbit.

David H. Moore is principal analyst in the Natural Resources and Commerce Division of the Congressional Budget Office. His professional concerns include science, technology, and space. He has followed space programs for years and has prepared key studies on space transportation and budget constraints on space programs.

Alex Roland teaches military history and the history of technology at Duke University. He has written widely on NASA history including books on space and aviation.

Marcia S. Smith is a specialist in aerospace policy for the Congressional Research Service of the Library of Congress. She has written widely on space programs for the U.S. Congress and has a special interest in the Soviet space program.

Jeffrey Struthers is vice president of the Center for Space and Advanced Technology where he works on space commercialization. Previously he directed the unit responsible for NASA programs in the Office of Management and Budget.

M. Mitchell Waldrop is a member of the news staff of *Science* magazine. He has covered a range of science and space policy issues including Landsat commercialization and artificial intelligence.

Albert D. Wheelon has had a distinguished career in government and industry which has spanned space activities from intelligence satellites to commercial communications satellites. Recently he retired as chairman of the board of Hughes Aircraft Corporation.

INTRODUCTION

Radford Byerly, Jr.

...THE SWIFTER THE PACE OF CHANGE, THE MORE LOVINGLY MEN
HAD TO CARE FOR AND CRITICIZE THEIR INSTITUTIONS TO KEEP
THEM INTACT THROUGH THE TURBULENT PASSAGES.

JOHN GARDNER

This volume brings many voices to a reconsideration of civilian
space policy. All the chapters taken together make the case for
changes and adaptation in -- and thus a fundamental
reconsideration of -- United States civilian space policy. The
theme is crystallized in Brewer's essay: "Change inevitably forces
NASA, and other once 'perfect places', to adapt."

This volume was assembled to meet a perceived need for open
and informed debate on space policy -- where "open" means that
all positions, decisions and assumptions are open to question --
because this is the best if not the only way to strengthen our
national space program.[1]

The *sine qua non* for a sound policy is a vigorous community
of *independent* space policy analysts to carry on and stimulate
debate. They must remain analysts to be credible critics. If they
made policy, they would have to defend it. It is hoped that this
volume will stimulate debate and catalyze a policy analysis
community.

The title -- *Space Policy Reconsidered* -- is meant to be
descriptive: That is, the intention is to

-- suspend automatic or uncritical acceptance of conventional
wisdom;

2

-- pursue an open agenda and open questions;
-- discuss realistic alternatives to business-as-usual; and
-- examine programs without attempting to promote or justify
   them.

Thus this volume is meant to challenge rather than confront
the present U.S. space program. Its approach is candid, frank, and
questioning in the honored American style of Lincoln and
Truman.

POINT OF DEPARTURE

The broad point of departure for this volume is support for a
vigorous space program including a strong human element, but not
blanket support to any given program, proposal, or policy.
Because the nation faces tough choices, workable space policy
requires reflection on realities, not simply faith in a "Vision" nor
resigned, tacit acceptance of someone else's vision. The latter is
unfortunately typical of some space scientists: if there is only one
game in town many will play it.

Born in reaction to Sputnik, the U.S. space program sometimes
has been driven more by considerations of national prestige in a
competitive world than by technical and scientific substance.[2]
Especially with the Soviets experiencing their own difficulties it is
becoming clearer that perception of the Soviet space threat will
wax and wane, and should not be counted on to stimulate or
sustain the flow of resources into the U.S. civilian space program.

The U.S. space program involves tens of thousands of highly
motivated and talented people. Many are working well past the
age of voluntary retirement because they believe in the program
and want to see it on-track again. But the program itself is far
from perfect. A healthy and effective point of view is stated in the
Congressional report on the Challenger accident:

> Perhaps it is arrogant to dissect and interrogate
> relentlessly projects and programs that bring home
> repeated A's for achievement and accomplishment.
> However, all of us...have learned from the Challenger
> tragedy that it is wisdom to do so, and it is a reflection
> of respect for the human fallibility that we all possess.[3]

In sum, the point of departure is the assumption that fair and
rigorous policy analysis will benefit the U.S. space program *and* its
principal agent, NASA; that we are wiser to try to understand our

shortcomings, and that through such effort we can gain a stronger, more resilient program.

TWO SPACE POLICY PARADIGMS

Why is there almost no tradition of independent space policy analysis? OTA has found that "The number of professionals engaged in space policy analysis is extremely small."[4] Why so few? Why is there such a small community if there is a community at all?

Perhaps by sharpening the questions the answers will begin to appear: Why is there so little receptivity for, and such a lack of understanding of, independent space policy analysis? Why should the motives of a policy analyst be questioned?[5] Is now the time "to get the critics off NASA's back?"[6] And why the biting tone in several of the chapters in this volume? Perhaps the answers lie in the fact that there are two contrasting ways of viewing the space program; one historically and currently dominant and another just emerging in volumes such as this one. The two are so different that adherents of each often find mutual understanding and communication to be difficult. What is the currently dominant paradigm?

PRESENT AND PAST: THE APOLLO PARADIGM

Today's paradigm sees our space program as the manifestation of a vision -- the vision that our human destiny is to explore the universe. NASA is keeper of the vision. Given the vision, analysis is not needed. Indeed analysis may present a threat to the vision. For reasons that will be clear, we call the institutional culture and assumptions derived from the vision the "Apollo Paradigm."

The Apollo Paradigm developed from the nation's cold war reaction to Sputnik which was so vividly portrayed by Wolfe[7]. In the paradigm NASA is a model "can-do" agency conducting the Apollo program. America had set out to put a human on the Moon and NASA accomplished the task spectacularly well. Most of the nation saw the Moon landings as a dramatic conclusion. The Apollo Paradigm saw them as the beginning of fulfillment of an even broader vision; a beginning that would lead to orbiting space stations, settlements on the Moon, and colonies on Mars. America was destined to lead the human race into space and it was NASA's job to show the way[8].

The Apollo Paradigm puts a premium on spectacular human space missions for both philosophical and practical reasons.

Philosophically, this aspect of the program realizes the broader vision of space exploration. Practically, the focus on sending people into space is thought to solidify public and political support for space funding and provides program engineers with their most stimulating and technically challenging tasks.[9]

In this paradigm the challenge that stimulates is the challenge to build large, advanced, complex spaceflight machines, preferably involving human crews, and to launch them successfully. Thus, from the Apollo perspective, the Shuttle is a great technical success;[10] any suggestion that science is a driver of space programs is characterized as a "myth;"[11] and human spaceflight is important in its own right -- thus perhaps "permanent presence" alone could justify the proposed Space Station. A central assumption is that only large missions with human crews, i.e. "spectaculars," can secure the political support and deliver the resources needed to advance the vision.

Under the Apollo Paradigm NASA's role as "keeper of the vision"[12] allows little room for dissent because disagreement amounts to disavowal of the vision. There is no room for penny-pinching. Attainment of the vision is the overriding objective and costs are a secondary consideration. The vision thus lessens the need for planning and evaluation -- resources and room to work are all that's needed. From this perspective policy analysis is not generally helpful and can be disruptive if it causes dissent, for everyone must work together harmoniously.

The vision, the harmony, and the concentration on hardware characteristic of this paradigm have enabled NASA to act decisively, to generate results, to achieve truly remarkable technical successes. Thus, like any other program, the civil space program does need vision. Its virtues are initiative, decisiveness, direction, focus, internal consensus, and enthusiasm -- all qualities needed to keep a program forging ahead.

But times have changed. "Ahead" may not be the same point on the compass. Merely keeping the screws turning and the rudder amidship is not likely to complete the voyage. New qualities are needed: a broader perspective which looks beyond technological achievement to economic, political, and cultural realities. As a nation we must not ignore the context of space policy -- we need a realistic appreciation of the environment which conditions and often drives or limits space policy.

For example, it is clear that President Kennedy's decision to go to the Moon was much more his solution to a political problem than a rendezvous with destiny.[13] Another example: With 20-20 hindsight it is clear that we made the wrong choice and that a broader-based policy analysis would have precluded the U.S. putting all its eggs in the Shuttle basket. That is, although there was a great deal of analysis of the Shuttle program, the common-sense criterion of not relying on a single launch system seems to have gotten lost among the details. And without the consequent pressure to capture all payloads, i.e. to keep flying, the program may have stopped to understand and correct the known problem with the O-rings.

FUTURE: THE POST-CHALLENGER PARADIGM

The essence of the Post-Challenger Paradigm is a more rigorously critical look at the space program. Prior to the accident the majority of Congress, the media, policy analysts, and the public were content with optimism and believed that the program that put men on the moon would succeed in whatever it tried,[14] although there was some sense of drift, i.e. that perhaps the program lacked direction.[15]

The Challenger explosion on January 28, 1986 thrust the space program into a wholly different and unfamiliar light. No longer infallible, it was now under intense scrutiny in almost every dimension. Through Congressional hearings and various reports, revelations of mismanagement and poor policymaking revealed an unfamiliar side of the U.S. space program.[16]

Almost overnight, obvious questions became inescapable: Why did the U.S. rely solely on the Shuttle? Why are human crews used to launch communication satellites? Why are science missions and the human spaceflight program tied together? What is the rationale for the Station? Such critical but ultimately useful questions of policy evaluation are at the core of the Post-Challenger Paradigm. This perspective recognizes that vision has its place and purpose, but that in today's environment vision must be tempered with reality -- the reality of resource constraints, the reality of international competition and cooperation, the reality of the impact of the human spaceflight program, especially the spectaculars, on other space activities, and the reality of accidents.

Thus, the Post-Challenger Paradigm is not focused on a particular mission but on rational application of resources, of projects evaluated against their promises, and of plans rooted in reality. This perspective begins by acknowledging the fact of a broad political mandate for sending humans into space but then insists that the implementation of that mandate be well-managed. In a democracy such support must be renewed by accomplishment, not consumed.

Therefore, in this paradigm resource constraints are acknowledged rather than dismissed.[17] If a vigorous space program, including a strong human element, is desired, the policy analyst seeks ways to have such a program by coping with political realities, e.g. by planning programs that can adapt to the kinds of changes that seem inevitable in our system, rather than blaming the system when the program fails.[18] The Post-Challenger Paradigm builds upon -- indeed it needs --the vision of the Apollo Paradigm in order to succeed in this new political context.

VISION AND ANALYSIS: BRINGING THE TWO CULTURES TOGETHER

Unfortunately even good policy analysts sometimes may be perceived to be querulous, irreverent, cynical, captious, or obstructive -- in other words at odds with an engineer with a job to do; an engineer working hard to implement a vision. And this goes far to explain the mutual discomfort and hostility.

But times are changing. As this is not an essay on such changes *per se*, let us merely list a few ways in which the context of today's space program is very different from the context of Apollo:

- -- funding is more constrained by our national deficit and the legislative response, Gramm-Rudman-Hollings;
- -- internationally there is a levelling of technical expertise, of economic resources, and of commitment to space so that the programs of other nations are increasingly relevant;
- -- many space science disciplines are maturing, putatively requiring more complex and expensive (and hence infrequent) missions;
- -- in the U.S. other government agencies are assuming a larger policy role;
- -- industry is trying to broaden its role from government contractor to entrepreneur; and
- -- in a broader social sense we seem to be approaching a crisis in government; there is a feeling that hard choices can no longer be postponed. At the same time the convergence of many social forces makes action difficult.

Is there a systematic difficulty? Are the communities of the two paradigms either not hearing each other or talking past each other so there is no realization that both vision and analysis are needed? Is there a lack of appreciation of the good faith of different points of view? John Gardner imagined our era from the perspective of the future:

> ...20th Century institutions were caught in a savage crossfire between uncritical lovers and unloving critics. On the one side, those who loved their institutions tended to smother them in an embrace of death, loving their rigidities more than their promise, shielding them from life-giving criticism. On the other side, there arose a breed of critics without love, skilled in demolition but untutored in the arts by which human institutions are nurtured and strengthened and made to flourish.

> Between the two, the institutions perished.

> ...scholars understood that where human institutions were concerned, love without criticism brings stagnation, and criticism without love brings destruction. And they emphasized that the swifter the pace of change, the more lovingly men had to care for and criticize their institutions to keep them intact through the turbulent passages.

> In short, men must be discriminating appraisers of their society, knowing coolly and precisely what it is about the society that thwarts or limits them -- and therefore needs modification. And so must they be discriminating protectors of their institutions, preserving those features that nourish and strengthen them and make them more free. To fit themselves for such tasks, they must be sufficiently serious to study their institutions, sufficiently dedicated to become expert in the art of modifying them.[19]

The policy analysis community thus has a solemn duty -- to become expert in the art of constructive modifications. That is what the Post-Challenger Paradigm is all about. This volume is offered as a contribution by loving critics and critical lovers to vigorous policy debate, and as a step toward the development of a functioning, independent policy community.

NOTES

1. A trenchant case for independent policy analysis is made (especially in the last paragraphs) by R. Garwin, "National Security Space Policy" *International Security*, Spring, 1987, p. 165.

8

2. This is a recurring theme in W. McDougal ...*the Heavens and the Earth/A Political History of the Space Age* (New York: Basic Books, 1985). See especially Chapter 17, "Benign Hypocrisy: American Space Diplomacy."

3. Committee on Science and Technology, U.S. House of Representatives, 99th Congress, *Investigation of the Challenger Accident*, House Report 99-1016 (Washington, D.C.: October 29, 1986) (hereafter "House Accident Report"), p. 7.

4. Office of Technology Assessment, *Civilian Space Stations and the U.S. Future in Space* (Washington, D.C.: U.S. Congress, OTA, 1984), p. 46.

5. For example, see the letter by NASA Administrator James Fletcher, *Science* (July 18, 1986), p. 263, in response to J. Logsdon, "The Space Shuttle Program: A Policy Failure?" *Science* (May 30, 1986), p. 1099.

6. James C. Fletcher, "Excerpts from Remarks Prepared for Delivery: National Space Club; February 24, 1988; Washington, D.C." (Washington, D.C.: NASA, 1988).

7. T. Wolfe, *The Right Stuff* (New York: Bantam Books, 1980).

8. H. Newell, *Beyond the Atmosphere* (Washington, D.C.: NASA History Series, NASA, 1980), p. 397.

9. Challenging technical frontiers is embedded in NASA's charter. Established by the National Aeronautics and Space Act of 1958 (42 U.S.C. 2451 et seq.), NASA is managed and largely staffed by engineers. The 1958 Act gives the agency eight objectives. The first ("...expansion of human knowledge...") is scientific but the weight of the others is toward technology development and applied science, i.e. engineering. The technical pattern was set by Apollo which was overwhelmingly an engineering program.

10. J. Fletcher, Proceedings of the Fourth National Space Symposium, U.S. Space Foundation, April, 1988, Colorado Springs, CO, p. 160. "To be sure, the Shuttle has done what it was meant to do; it remains the most versatile, flexible, and useful flying machine in the world."

11. B. Bova, letter to *Science* (August 8, 1987), p. 610.

12. C. Matlack, "The Space Program's Mid-Life Crisis" *Government Executive* (October 1988), p. 16, Quoting Alan Ladwig, director of special projects, NASA Office of Exploration.

13. See McDougal (note 2) especially Chapter 15, "Destination Moon." Also J. Logsdon, *The Decision to Go to the Moon* (Chicago: University of Chicago Press, 1970).

14. See, for example (a) R. Rosenblatt, "Aiming High in '81" *Time* (January 12, 1981), p. 8. "Like the U.S., the space shuttle Columbia is looking up as the year begins." (b) House Accident Report (note 3), p. 7. "We as a Committee have perhaps exhibited the human inclination to accept the successful completion of a flight or event as an indication of the overall strength of all aspects of its planning and execution."

15. There were questions about U.S. space policy direction before the accident. Again, there are many possible references. Two are: (a) Editors, "Adrift in Space" *N.Y. Times* (January 7, 1986) "...NASA...seems to have lost its sense of direction." (b) D. Granat, "Search for a Space Policy: Space Issues Before Congress Involve Setting New Projects, Meeting Foreign Challenge" *Congressional Quarterly* (July 24, 1982), p. 1763. Granat refers to "...the absence of overall agreement within the federal government about the future direction of the U.S. civilian space program."

16. See, for example: Stuart Diamond, "NASA Wasted Billions, Federal Audits Disclose" *New York Times* (April 23, 1986), p. 1. Also, Diamond, "NASA Cut or Delayed Safety Spending" *New York Times* (April 24, 1986), p. 1.

17. In response to a question referring to NASA's budget problems and the reality of expecting full funding as Congress tries to meet Gramm-Rudman limits, NASA Administrator Fletcher said there is no problem except for the artificial one of NASA's budget being part of the small discretionary fraction of the budget. He further said that NASA's program priorities are the true realities in this most crucial year. American Institute of Aeronautics and Astronautics Annual Meeting, May 3, 1988, Arlington, VA, from author's notes of the meeting. The same flavor is contained in "Excerpts from remarks prepared for delivery" by Fletcher at the AIAA meeting and released by the NASA Public Affairs Office.

18. For example, see the letter by NASA Administrator James Fletcher in response to the Logsdon article (note 5).

19. John W. Gardner, "Uncritical Lovers and Unloving Critics," remarks at the 100th Commencement of Cornell University, Ithaca, New York, June 1, 1968.

PART ONE

Overviews: Setting a Context

The civilian space program is clearly in a period of transition. The Challenger accident, and the long disruptive recovery from its effects, will cast a shadow for years to come. Picking up the pieces provides a major challenge for NASA and other leaders of the U.S. civilian space program.

The next few years will be a very active ones in space. But where in a broader sense is the program going? Where should it be going? What lessons should the United States learn from the recent history of the program and more particularly how can the future policy and program directions fit into the broader context of American society in the coming decade?

Such issues and concerns are addressed in the first three chapters. The authors come to their assessments from different backgrounds and different perspectives but they share a concern that the historical evolution of the U.S. space program has placed an increasingly heavy emphasis on large engineering and development projects to the possible detriment of the productivity and effectiveness of the overall effort. They set a context for more specific contributions in later chapters.

David H. Moore, a senior analyst in the Congressional Budget Office, sees the future civilian space program coming into conflict with an increasingly difficult budget climate: "Barring a change in the priority Congress grants NASA's program, the program and the budget deficit are on a collision course." Consequently, unless there is a significant increase in the NASA budget in the next several years, the Nation faces hard choices that go to the very heart of the program emphasis that has evolved in response to Sputnik and the competition with the Soviets for world leadership in the manned exploration of space. Moore believes that the very large investments made by the U.S. in space capabilities during the 1970s and 1980s have "left the program in a position to generate significant benefits" in the coming decade and beyond.

Alex Roland, a military historian, presents a fascinating and provocative interpretation of why the U.S. continues to pursue a grand vision of man-in-space despite the budgetary and program realities that might suggest a more constrained and cautious approach. He believes that we may be coming to the end of an era in manned space flight; that the Challenger accident was most likely the "defining event;" and that the end of the "romantic era of spaceflight" has yet to be appreciated by policymakers, especially the current leadership of NASA.

The final context chapter is from a senior statesman of the American space community. Albert D. Wheelon provides a tour-de-force survey of current civilian space policy issues. Wheelon's discussion is especially compelling because he has been a practitioner of the art of planning and building real spacecraft as the former Chief Executive Officer of the world's leading manufacturer of commercial communications and military satellites. His statement is impressive for its wisdom about the technical and political-administrative factors that influence real-world decisions in the space program. It is also a model of clarity in addressing major issues that continue to trouble the civilian space program.

Although these authors approach their topics from diverse perspectives, they share a belief in the promises of space and a strong desire to enhance the future of the program. A common thread running through these essays is the need to adopt new ways of thinking if the program is to succeed in a challenging environment.

Chapter 1

A BUDGET-CONSTRAINED NASA PROGRAM FOR THE 1990s

David H. Moore[1]

HOUSTON, WE HAVE A PROBLEM HERE.

JACK SWIGERT
APOLLO 13

In January of 1988 the President requested that Congress grant NASA a $2.5 billion increase for 1989 over its 1988 appropriation level of $9.0 billion. This increase was earmarked to develop the Space Station, to continue to repair the damage done to the Shuttle system by the Challenger accident, and to carry forward other parts of NASA's plan for the nation's civilian space program. The request for an increase of nearly 30 percent, while substantial in and of itself, appeared particularly large in light of the October 1987 deficit reduction agreement that restricted overall spending growth to only two percent above the 1988 level. As the appropriation process moved through the summer, it was clear that Congress would not grant NASA the full request, but that an increase of almost $1.7 billion, 19 percent higher than the 1988 level, would be forthcoming.

While the 1989 appropriation temporarily relieves budgetary pressures, particularly for the Space Station program, it also highlights the lack of fiscal certainty in NASA's budget over the next few years. To implement its program, NASA could require a real dollar budget level of $14.5 billion (1988 dollars)[*] annually

---

[*] Hereafter all dollar figures refer to 1988 dollars unless otherwise stated.

by the early 1990s.[2] If NASA is to realize its long held vision of continuous human operation in low earth orbit it must win these increases in a budget environment dominated by pressure to cut the federal deficit. Because the outcome of the debate about how important a spending priority the NASA program should be is not a foregone conclusion -- NASA could be restricted to its current budget level -- it is reasonable to ask the following questions: What would the civilian space program look like were NASA restricted to its current budget level of $10 billion annually during the 1990s? What criteria would be used to select its programs and to formulate its policies? What opportunities can be taken advantage of during the next decade, and what opportunities would be foregone or delayed well into the next century?

NASA'S CORE PROGRAM AND THE FEDERAL DEFICIT

NASA's program for the 1990s will require real increases in its budget. Meeting the goals of the Balanced Budget and Emergency Deficit Control Reaffirmation Act of 1987, or Gramm-Rudman-Hollings, will require some combination of reduced spending or increased taxes that lowers the annual federal deficit to zero by 1993 from its 1988 level of about $150 million.[3] Barring a change in the priority Congress grants NASA's program, the program and the budget deficit are on a collision course.

The *National Journal* recently emphasized the extent to which the deficit dominates the environment in which NASA will seek to increase its share of federal spending:

For Washington the deficit has become an all-consuming problem of perhaps unprecedented proportions. It establishes limits, if not straitjackets, for policymakers in the White House, Congress, and the private sector.[4]

For 1989 the deficit target of $136 billion plus a $10 billion margin for error was barely met. The Office of Management and Budget estimates the deficit to be $144 billion, a mere $2 billion, the equivalent of .002 percent of federal outlays, below the "sequester trigger" of $146 billion.[5] Had the sequester trigger been squeezed, federal spending would have been cut "across the board," except that 75 percent of the $1.1 trillion board, including interest on the national debt, domestic entitlement, and roughly two thirds of the defense budget is exempted, and thus would be unavailable for cutting. NASA's budget of $10.7 billion is part of the remaining 25 percent of the budget that would have been cut to lower the deficit to the target level. Put in another way, under current law, NASA's less than one percent of federal spending becomes four percent of the pie in the event that the sequester knife is applied.

But if the 1989 budget debate is history, what does the future look like? The Congressional Budget Office projects that under current budget policies -- no change in tax law and current spending levels increased only for inflation -- the deficit will be substantially greater than that permitted by law for each of the next five years. The deficit gap to be filled by spending reductions or tax increases is estimated to be $36 billion in 1990, $67 billion in 1991, $98 billion in 1992 and $121 billion in 1993.[6] Any increase in federal spending for a particular program, without an offsetting decrease in spending elsewhere or a tax increase, will increase the gap between the deficit and the sequester triggers.[7]

That NASA will be among the agencies seeking such increases is a near certainty. Figure 1 presents the real dollar level of NASA's spending and its composition in the post-Apollo era and a projection of the real dollar cost of NASA's core program through 2000.[8] The decline in the nation's resource commitment to space during the 1970s is clear, as NASA's budget falls from $12 billion in 1970 to around $7.0 billion in 1975, remaining at this level until the rise in real expenditures to around $10.5 billion at the end of the Reagan years. The projected steep increase in the NASA budget necessary to support its program is driven by the Space Station and the space transportation investment necessary to support the station's construction and subsequent operation on orbit.[9] Since the end of the Apollo program NASA has pursued its goal of human exploration of space by developing a transportation system, the Space Shuttle, to replace the Apollo-generation launch vehicles and by proposing to build a permanently manned Space Station. During the 1970s NASA's investment priority was the development of the Space Shuttle. By 1982 NASA had spent $30 billion to develop, build, and operate the Space Shuttle system.[10] Through the first twenty five flights into 1988, including the replacement for Challenger and the Department of Defense's investment in the "slick six" shuttle launch complex at Vandenberg Air Force Base (a facility that is currently mothballed), the total national expenditures on the Shuttle system are above $50 billion.[11]

Concurrent with Space Shuttle development, NASA initiated the Tracking and Data Relay Satellite system (TDRS) program in the late 1970s. This system was designed as a communications and tracking network to replace the Apollo-generation ground

16

Figure 1:
NASA Budget: Historical and Projected

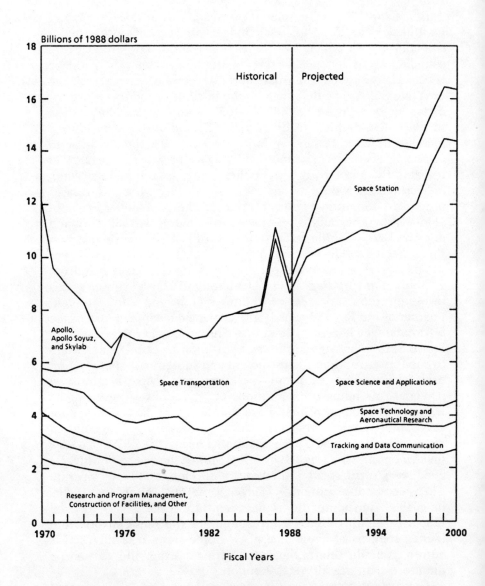

Billions of 1988 dollars

Historical | Projected

Space Station

Apollo,
Apollo Soyuz,
and Skylab

Space Transportation

Space Science and Applications

Space Technology and
Aeronautical Research

Tracking and Data Communication

Research and Program Management,
Construction of Facilities, and Other

Fiscal Years

SOURCE: Congressional Budget Office, *The NASA Core Program in the 1990s and Beyond*, p. 17 (May, 1988).

stations in the tracking and guidance of human space flight, and as a conduit for the anticipated large volume of data flowing to Earth from human and automated activities in Earth orbit.

Other investments, largely complementary, were made in the space science program, including instruments and equipment to be flown on the Shuttle, and two long lived orbiting observatories -- the Hubble Space Telescope and the Gamma Ray Observatory -- and several major planetary probes, foremost among them the billion dollar plus Galileo mission to Jupiter. Literally, tens of billions of dollars of investment have yet to be fully exploited. The major operational task for NASA over the next five years is to reap the benefits of these investments made during the 1970s and 1980s.

The goals of launching and operating these missions and operating supporting infrastructure systems is a starting point in understanding the future budgetary requirements of the NASA program. Operating the Shuttle system could cost $2 billion annually.[12] The bulk of these costs are fixed, meaning they do not vary as the Shuttle system flies additional flights.[13] Continued investments in both large and small improvements in the Shuttle system could run as high as $2.5 billion in a peak year in the early 1990s. Tracking and data communications expenditures are projected to be $1 billion annually. In the space science area, operating and maintaining the Hubble Space Telescope and the Gamma Ray Observatory could run $150 million annually. Despite the Challenger accident NASA's plan remains vulnerable to major disruptions in the TDRS and Shuttle systems, yet dramatic changes in these activities would require substantial additional spending or the continuing and expensive deferral of the benefits of currently grounded missions.

NASA's plan also calls for new investments in the early 1990s, most prominently the continuously inhabited Space Station scheduled for launch in the mid 1990s. The final 1989 budget included just under $900 million for the Space Station program. These costs could grow to 3.5 billion by 1993.[14] New investments in space science and applications programs are also part of NASA's plan for the 1990s. The most costly of these missions are two additional orbiting observatories, automated exploration of Saturn and the asteroid belt, and a comprehensive project to monitor the Earth's environmental system. These and other space science projects could raise the space science and applications budget from $1.7 billion in 1989 to 2.2 billion in the mid 1990s.

The NASA program and the Federal deficit pull NASA's budget in opposite directions. The program requires a larger budget, but lowering the deficit will likely require reduced spending with or without an increase in taxes. Nevertheless, as the increase of $1.7 billion dollars for 1989 indicates, the political system could grant the space program higher priority and the resources to implement NASA's plan. Should it do so, a clear blueprint exists to guide the program during the 1990s. The same can not be said if NASA is restricted to its current budget level of roughly $10 billion.

POSSIBLE CRITERIA FOR A $10 BILLION SPACE PROGRAM

At least four criteria could serve as guidelines in designing a NASA program that could fit within a $10 billion annual budget between now and the end of the century. While these criteria are not a substitute for formal cost-benefit analysis or the type of optimization favored by economic analysis, they may prove useful in light of large uncertainties in calculating costs and benefits of the civilian space program, and the value of the NASA program inputs and outputs.[15] The criteria draw upon the recent experience of the NASA program, and find their origin in a critique of that experience. They suggest that a budget constrained NASA program for the 1990s must:

-- have *continuity* with the post-Apollo effort to develop and operate a low earth infrastructure, as the inertia of the past twenty years has created opportunities to gain substantial returns for relatively small current expenditures, despite the failure of major parts of the program to live up to their advanced billing;
-- be *realistic* in its estimation of program cost and schedule, and its expectations for the performance of the systems involved;
-- be *responsive* to broad national needs beyond those of the space community; and finally,
-- pursue *institutional innovations* in the process of selecting investment projects, in determining their scale of operation, and in their actual operation.

The first and the last criteria seem to point in different directions. The Shuttle system has been the subject of considerable criticism since the Challenger accident; indeed, it has been suggested that the Shuttle program be abandoned. Continuity suggests that the scales be tipped towards the Shuttle system and the future expenditures necessary to test the central claim of the Shuttle's advocates; namely, that the constellation of infrastructure and missions designed and developed in the 1970s can produce better more cost-effective science, technology and applications than the currently available alternatives. However, the widening interest in space as an environment necessary to provide important public goods and, potentially, private profits, requires that current operations and future investments be guided more by "market oriented" processes of choice than by NASA's traditional, centrally planned approach. Too many different interests and constituencies depend on space activity to allow the next round of investment decisions to be made exclusively by NASA.

The possibility of an overall budget limit is not the only reality NASA may be forced to face as it examines its program for the 1990s. Increased attention should be focused on the product the program delivers. Thus, the program elements of a $10 billion space program need to be well-conceived and brought in on schedule at estimated cost. Furthermore, the future degree of interdependence among projects should be limited in recognition of the risk that the entire program could be paralyzed by an event like the Challenger accident.

The need to produce a continuing stream of output -- scientific results, technical progress, and other public goods -- is a key element of a responsive space program. The current NASA program is responsive to the long-held agenda of the space community that calls for extensive and near-term human exploration of space. If this agenda could be accomplished at NASA's current funding level, perhaps little more would be necessary. The half of the populace that see human space exploration as important could be reconciled with the seventy percent that say the nation spends about the right amount or too much on the NASA program. However, the program's claim to increased real dollar resources, at a time when spending priorities are being questioned, requires that NASA's agenda be responsive to the concerns of a broader national audience. Among these concerns are the competitiveness of U.S. industry in international markets and the delivery of public goods, for example environmental monitoring, that have a tangible effect on the quality of life on Earth.

Continuity

NASA's current program was born in the post-Apollo era. The Challenger accident has had the effect of slowing its progress and increasing its cost, but has not changed its basic thrust. That thrust can best be described as the creation and exploitation of an infrastructure capable of supporting manned and unmanned operations in low earth orbit for the purposes of space science, applications, technology demonstration and, ultimately, manned exploration of the solar system and beyond. Suggesting continuity as a criteria to guide the formulation of a productive $10 billion space program does not require acceptance of the entire NASA agenda, nor does it hold that sunk costs are a justification for throwing good money after bad. Rather, the continuity criterion recognizes that the life cycle of costs and benefits of the investments made in the 1970s and early 1980s has left the program in a position to generate significant benefits at lower costs than alternatives.

A major difference between the current NASA program and that of the Apollo era is the type of investments made, and the life cycle of their costs and benefits. The Apollo effort rose and fell in little more than a decade, with all costs and most benefits occurring over that time period. The post-Apollo program strategy has been to make investments that in an early phase require large investment expenditures in the design, development and production of a system, balanced only by the benefits of concurrent technical spin-offs. Subsequently, after this long period of gestation, benefits are delivered as the capital facilities are operated and operating costs are incurred. Thus, the low earth infrastructure investments made during the 1970s and 1980s were conceived of as integral parts of the U.S. civilian program well into the next century, providing benefits over their operating life -- scientific knowledge and other public goods -- in exchange for continuing operating costs.[16]

It is current and future operating costs, not the sunk cost of capital investments made in specific missions and the supporting infrastructure, that are relevant to the question of whether to continue or deviate from the current course. Admittedly, the Shuttle system in particular has performed far below the claims of its promoters. Yet, in the final calculation even with only a limited cargo carrying role, the Shuttle may prove equal to the test of cost-benefit analysis. Alternatives to the current program that eliminated manned activities, even were they culturally feasible, would require spending to redesign those payloads currently designed for Shuttle launch only and, forgoing or dramatically changing activities that are currently designed to take advantage of the presence of a human operator. Other alternatives that seek to substitute a new manned system for the

Shuttle would themselves require significant new investment. The cost of operating the Shuttle as currently anticipated by NASA may in fact represent the best course when measured against the system's unique ability to deliver the benefits of carrying cargo and providing a platform for scientific activity.

Realism

In the wake of the Challenger accident the realism of virtually every element of the NASA program has been questioned. Even prior to the accident an air of unreality pervaded discussions of major NASA enterprises, from the Shuttle system's flight rate to the Space Station's cost. As a criterion for program design realism is pertinent in at least three areas: 1) the cost, schedule and performance expectations for individual projects or missions, 2) the degree of interdependence in the program as a whole, and 3) the need to balance the program's mix of piloted and unpiloted missions.

It is the conventional wisdom that the eventual outcome of a typical civilian space project will be a less capable and more costly system delivered at a date later than initially anticipated. A recently completed General Accounting Office review of major space science projects confirms this wisdom, with costs of the Galileo and Hubble Space Telescope projects running a billion dollars over original estimates.[17] These overruns are caused by a complex set of interactions among the technical characteristics of the projects themselves, the infrastructure they require, and the budget process.

A measure of the success of the space program is the widening scientific interest in using the space environment to create new knowledge. Solar system exploration has been joined by physics, chemistry and, more recently, biology as disciplines that benefit from space-based activity. Concomitantly, as individual disciplines have moved forward, the scale of facilities necessary to produce new results has grown larger, requiring both substantial short term development spending and lower, but longer term, operating expenditures to realize the desired scientific result. For example, the first generation infrared astronomy spacecraft, IRAS, was an inexpensive mission limited to one year in orbit. Its successor, the Space Infrared Telescope will cost over a billion dollars and be in operation for at least ten years with annual operating costs in the neighborhood of $50 million.[18] Thus, a trend has been established of more areas of inquiry seeking support for increasingly complicated and costly missions.

Within the budget process no compelling incentives exist for truth in budgeting. The interactions among the agency and its network of contractors and scientific constituents, the rest of the executive branch and the Congress work more smoothly when everyone's project is included in the program. Faced with a tight fiscal environment, only optimistic cost and schedule projections, and exaggerated performance claims allow everyone's project to be in the program. A proliferation of missions to serve more scientific disciplines and applications, and large investment projects give the program as a whole the appearance of vigor and breadth. Yet, as optimistic scenarios can be realized for only some, but not all projects, the program as a whole is vulnerable to a dynamic of cost overruns -- schedule stretch-outs -- deferred benefits. Once started, this sequence can spread from one project to the next and, ultimately, engulf the program as a whole.

If a project overruns its estimated cost, it rebounds against the implicit budget ceiling requiring unanticipated funding or a stretch-out. If a stretch-out is accepted, the overrun will grow in the project where the original escalation occurred. Under either assumption the presence of a budget ceiling assures the spread of the original overrun to other projects, invariably leading to a schedule stretch-out -- cost overrun -- deferred benefits sequence in these projects. As more space science projects become open-ended rather than discrete (e.g. like the Hubble Space Telescope, which has a long operational life at substantial cost), curtailing operating expenditures for existing facilities to meet development overruns in new projects could become an attractive, but ultimately self-defeating, option, in that the return to previous investment requires the use of these investments. The future productivity of the program would not be enhanced if, for example, the Hubble Space Telescope operations were curtailed in order to fund the development of the Space Infrared Telescope.

These budget dynamics are intensified to the extent that the mission oriented elements of NASA's program are themselves dependent on infrastructure facilities that are in development and, therefore, exposed to considerable technical risk. The Galileo mission to Jupiter, when originally formulated in the late 1970s, was dependent upon an untested booster stage -- the Shuttle -- and an untested upper stage. A large part of the billion dollar escalation in the cost of the mission is the consequence of problems in these elements of infrastructure rather than the mission itself. In this context the overruns caused by the Challenger accident represent an extreme but not a unique event.

Realism will require acceptance by all of the parties in the policy making process that space activity is not cheap. In a budget constrained world it will also require assignment of priorities not only at the program level but in limiting the breadth of the program as a whole. It could be that the most productive U.S. space program is one with a narrowed, intensified focus rather than a broader less intense reach. Finally, realism requires a portfolio of activities diversified with regard to its dependence on specific pieces of infrastructure. In the first instance this means providing funding for a mixed fleet of launch vehicles to lessen dependence on the Shuttle system. In the future it may mean forgoing very large expensive missions in favor of several smaller but independent missions.

A continuing role for manned space flight is also an outcome of a realistic appraisal of the role of the civilian space program in American culture. Utilitarian arguments in support of piloted space flight are difficult, if not impossible, to support in a limited cost-benefit analysis. Human presence is expensive and automated substitutes abound in most proven applications of space technology. Even in materials processing, an area where the ability to innovate and improvise is valued, humans may ultimately have more costs than benefits. Yet, in the public perception, the NASA program is equated with human space flight and it is a program attribute for which there is a willingness to pay. Thus, while a budget constrained program for NASA may shift the balance of human and automated space activity towards the latter, human space flight must be a given in any feasible program reconstruction.

Responsiveness

The drive to extend a human presence beyond the Earth is the fundamental imperative to which the NASA program responds. At times other goals pull at the resources of the agency, but essentially manned space flight and its logical consequence, human exploration, dominates the NASA agenda. The post-Apollo vision of NASA program is framed by the manned Shuttle and the manned Space Station and, ultimately manned planetary exploration. Even the parts of the space science community that do not require manned space flight often express support for the manned effort because, the argument goes, without people in space automated activities would not be supported at all. In the 1960s this objective fit well with, and was responsive to, an apparent national need to demonstrate the superiority of democratic capitalism over Soviet socialism. The systemic competition has moved on, NASA's program has not.

While NASA's pursuit of its primary goal may indeed benefit the nation, the current fiscal environment and the press of a number of more immediate issues should lead the civilian space program to respond to a broader set of concerns. These include U.S. competitiveness in international markets, the long-term health of the nation's technology base, and environmental monitoring. Responding to these concerns need not force NASA to abandon human exploration of outer space as a long term objective, but it could alter the balance of manned and unmanned activities in favor of the latter, and change NASA's near term investment priorities as they are evaluated against a $10 billion budget ceiling.

NASA's charter, the Space Act of 1958, clearly establishes its role as a developer and disseminator of technology to the private economy. The aeronautical research program is held by some observers to be the most effective part of the NASA program in this area. Other "applications" areas, such as, communication, navigation, and remote sensing have suffered as NASA has pursued its major objectives. As importantly, the very open-ended and admittedly risky space technology program -- a program devoted to the building blocks of systems like the Shuttle rather than the systems themselves -- continues in long term decline, despite the almost universally held view that much of what the United States does in space is built on a foundation of twenty-year old technology.[19]

In its search to justify the Space Station as the next logical step for the United States in space, NASA at one point, emphasized the potential contribution of the Space Station to the economy. Subsequently, this rationale went the way of its predecessors and was pushed to the background largely because the argument did not fit with the program. In looking at the whole NASA program and a $10 billion budget constraint it is programs that do not respond to sound rationales that must be restructured, discarded or postponed, not the rationales themselves.

Institutional Innovation

During the Apollo years NASA was essentially a project team. As its concerns have broadened so have its responsibilities. NASA has added the role of infrastructure operator to that of developer of technology and explorer. This transition has not always been smooth, and occurs at a time when the use of space for public and private purposes is expanding, bringing NASA into contact, and sometimes conflict, with a growing number of organizations. It is by no means certain that business as usual can continue. To this end a number of radical reorganizations have been proposed: privatizing, or "fencing" the Shuttle, the creation of independent space science institutes, private financing of all or part of the Space Station, to name a few. Yet, none of the simplistic solutions to reorganizing the institutions and processes by which the country gets it's business done in space are likely to be adopted in part because NASA's minimum agenda during the early 1990s is crowded with major missions that take priority over large scale institutional change. The pursuit of smaller scale institutional innovations should be on the agenda for the early 1990s, however. Policy makers need to know what systems and technologies can operate independent of the federal government, and how the infrastructure and technology decisions made in the federal space program can lead to better and more efficient operating systems.

Changing the institutional mechanisms that determine which infrastructure investments will be made, the characteristics of these investments and their scale of operation is a critical issue for the future. The current system is essentially a centrally planned one in which agency managers select large projects and then designs and scales of operation guided by the post-Apollo vision of the program and its overall objectives. "Users," those parts of the NASA program, other government agencies, and private parties who require infrastructure services such as transportation, manned or unmanned platforms, and tracking and data services, are consulted and at the margin influence the project design and scale with which they are presented in so far as these changes are consistent with the underlying manned exploration goal.

This system is not without its virtues. It has been forward looking in the scale of operation to which its aspires. It has not, however, resulted in rapid or cost effective progress in science and applications. Moreover, it provides only limited incentives for managers to introduce new technologies in that no competing alternative is open to federal government users. In case of the Shuttle, even prior to the Challenger accident, the scientific community waited for the Shuttle and then paid an implicitly higher price for its services than for the ELV alternative.[20] It is clear that without the preferences of NASA's central planners to push forward manned space transportation *per se*, no single user or group, public or private, would have been willing to pay a price

26

for space transportation sufficiently high to cover the cost of designing, producing and operating the current system.

A variety of proposals to change NASA's institutional structure use this outcome as a point of departure. The objective is to empower users by allowing them to choose how their infrastructure needs will be met and providing them with the financial support necessary to enforce their choice. For example, a few space science projects might be granted funding sufficient to cover transportation costs and allowed to procure that transportation from NASA's own space transportation group or the private sector. The virtue of this plan is that it allows users to have a greater say in the mix of space transportation currently available and in doing so provides a signpost to guide future investment decisions.

Several experiments in decision making are included in the current program. The Office of Commercial Program's Centers for the Commercial Development of Space provide settings that allow the private sector and universities to define their own microgravity research program. The recently unveiled National Space Policy directs NASA to procure services commercially wherever possible, rather than develop and operate public facilities. In the case of the former little can be said until flight opportunities are available. Concerning the latter vagueness and ideological axe grinding could be the enemies of successful experimentation.

As a criterion for program design, institutional innovation is less central in the immediate future than continuity, realism or responsiveness. Nevertheless if the premise is accepted that NASA will not control all civilian activities in low earth orbit and ultimately will be moving outward in its exploration mission, then it is important to find out what works in improving decision making and resource allocation.

PROGRAM OPTIONS

The four criteria and the $10 billion (1988 dollar) budget constraint require changes in the NASA program for the 1990s. The budget constraint certainly precludes the much-discussed new manned initiatives to the Moon or Mars, as these programs could require a NASA budget of $20 to $30 billion annually by the second half of the 1990s.[21] The budget constraint alone would not prevent NASA from stretching out its current program, however. Application of the criteria of continuity, realism, responsiveness and institutional innovation suggests that an alternative or restructured option is superior, however. The options of stretching out or restructuring NASA's program differ in the priority assigned to three parts of NASA's program: infrastructure investment, development and operations of missions taking advantage of the existing infrastructure, and investment in new space technology.

Stretching Out the Current Program

A stretched-out version of the current program involves delaying the Space Station until the end of the century, taking significant risks in the transportation systems necessary to support the project and, as a consequence, delaying the scientific and applications benefits anticipated from the Space Station program. The total cost of the Space Station would certainly increase as the development and construction schedules would be less than optimal. Transportation investments in major Shuttle improvements or even replacement orbiters also do not fit in the budget envelope. Funding would not be available to support a diversified space launch capacity for NASA, but NASA's demand for space transportation during the mid-1990s would decline as Space Station construction would be pushed back toward the turn of the century.

In space science, current funding levels could be maintained. New projects unrelated to the Space Station, for example the Automated X-Ray Astronomical Facility, the Space Infrared Telescope, and the Earth Observation System, would be vulnerable to the dynamic of schedule stretch-out -- cost overrun -- deferred benefits. No significant increase in applications support could be accommodated. The space technology program would be maintained at its current level, and the program as a whole would enter the next century with some forty-year-old technology.

A stretched out version of the current program would maintain continuity with NASA's vision of the early 1970s. It would be neither realistic nor responsive, however. The dynamic of schedule stretch out -- cost overrun -- deferred benefits could potentially spread like wildfire between Space Station and the rest of the program, and within the space science program. The exposure of the program to the risks of interdependence would be ever-present as the Shuttle would be NASA's sole access to space because budget limitations would not permit the procurement of expendable launch vehicles. Programs such as materials processing in space and life science would essentially mark time until the station was completed. Funding constraints would permit little in the way of institutional innovation.

A Restructured Program

The central premise of a restructured program is to deemphasize manned space flight. Instead the focus would be on unmanned science missions, for example, automated planetary exploration and earth monitoring, and rebuilding the space technology program. The Space Station program would be cancelled in favor of a combination of more spacelab flights, a man-tended platform -- physically similar to the proposed commercially developed space facility -- and extended duration flights of the Shuttle orbiter. Like the stretched-out program option, new investment in space transportation to carry people could not be funded. However, sufficient funding would be available to support five or six Shuttle flights a year and procurement of expendable launch vehicle services to support space science and applications launch demand.

Space science, applications and technology could receive considerably more funding under a restructured option than under a stretch-out. The distribution of this funding, beyond completing the current agenda, could be governed by the principle of responsiveness. Thus, at the margin, projects would be preferred that provide tangible public goods and directly strengthen the national technical base. Intensified earth monitoring would be a high priority mission.

The major discontinuity in the restructured option is in the Space Station program. The physical problem is less pressing than the institutional one. A man-tended platform that could be substituted for the more ambitious current station program would allow progress in microgravity experimentation -- a major Space Station activity -- but would not provide a laboratory to learn about the effect of long duration space flight on humans. Thus, at least a part of the Space Station mission could be accommodated. The international commitments to Europe and Japan represent a major institutional discontinuity, however. Were the current program cancelled U.S. prestige would invariably be hurt. All the U.S could offer would be international participation in its scaled back laboratory in low Earth orbit, and Shuttle support for the Space Station partner's missions on a full cost basis.

In terms of realism a restructured option for a $10 billion space program is superior to a stretch-out. The pressure of undertaking a highly visible investment program and at the same time producing tangible returns from previous investments would be relieved. Moreover, the commitment to use and fund a mixed fleet of space transportation vehicles would decrease the risks of interdependence. Finally, the increased funding permitted for basic technology programs would allow NASA to step forward from what many in the engineering community describe as a 1960s technology base.

GAINS AND LOSSES

The prospect of a budget constrained space program does not sit well with space enthusiasts. For this group, that holds human expansion into the stars to be a compelling priority of human destiny, the pace of the last twenty years has been appallingly slow. There is no scenario under which a budget constrained program provides substantial support for this goal. In relation to a more modest and near term set of goals, any version of a $10 billion space program would represent a step back from leadership in space activity. It is an overstatement to claim that the U.S. would be a second rate spacefaring nation: its automated space activities could be second to none. Moreover, it is unlikely that either Europe or Japan will have an independent manned space flight capability before the turn of the century. Nonetheless, the U.S. would clearly be second to the Soviet Union in manned space flight.

The trade-off forced by a $10 billion budget-constraint is between a program emphasizing infrastructure to support manned space flight and one emphasizing automated activities and technology development. The former would slow applications, science and technology development in favor of an infrastructure investment that would permit a continuing presence of U.S. citizens in low-Earth orbit around the turn of the century, but leaves these citizens with little to do, supported by a space program long on circus and short on bread. The latter would provide for leadership in limited areas, and revitalize the nation's space science and applications program and space technology base.

NOTES

1. The author is a Principal Analyst in the Natural Resources and Commerce Division of the Congressional Budget Office. The

30

views expressed in this essay are the author's own and do not represent the position of the Congressional Budget Office.

2. Congressional Budget Office, *The NASA Program in the 1990s and Beyond,* May 1988, ch. II.

3. Congressional Budget Office, *The Economic and Budget Outlook: An Update,* August 1988, p. ix.

4. Lawrence J. Haas, "The Deficit Culture," *National Journal,* June 4, 1988, p. 1460.

5. Office of Management and Budget, *Initial Sequester Report to the President and Congress for the Fiscal Year of 1989,* August 25, 1988, p. 3.

6. Congressional Budget Office, *The Economic and Budget Outlook,* p. xi.

7. A slowing of economic growth to recession levels would relax the deficit target requirements in any given year. While the Congressional Budget Office does not offer a forecast beyond 1989, the fact that the current expansion of the economy is six years old (the second longest since the end of the Second World War) leads the CBO to conclude that historical averages are consistent with, "... the occurrence of one mild recession..." some time in the early 1990s. Nevertheless, the dominating role of the deficit in current policy thinking make the odds far better than even that pressure to reduce the gap between spending and revenues will continue with or without a recession. See, Congressional Budget Office, *The Economic and Budget Outlook,* ch. I.

8. Congressional Budget Office, *The NASA Program for the 1990s and Beyond,* ch. 2, includes more detailed program descriptions and budget estimates for the version of the NASA program discussed below.

9. Congressional Budget Office, *NASA's Program for the 1990's and Beyond,* ch. II.

10. Congressional Budget Office, *Pricing Options for the Space Shuttle,* March 1985, p. 1.

11. The estimate of $50 billion national expenditures on the shuttle system through 1988 includes the $30 billion through 1982, an additional $3 billion each year 1983 through 1988 in the shuttle operations and shuttle production and operational capability accounts, $3 billion in Department of Defense investment, and $2.1 billion to replace the Challenger.

12. NASA alternatives to the shuttle system as a launch system for its science and applications payloads is limited in the near term by the availability of expendable launch vehicles (ELVs). This constraint reflects the lead time required to procure launch

services, the Department of Defense's near term demand for launch vehicles currently in production and NASA's unwillingness to free up resources to place orders for ELV's in the first year after the Challenger accident.

13. For a discussion of the nature of shuttle costs and of their implications for pricing policy see. Congressional Budget Office, *Pricing Options for the Space Shuttle*, ch. II.

14. The space station program is international in scope and includes a polar orbiting unmanned platform, the polar platform, as well as the more widely known continuously inhabited structure in a 28.5 degree orbit. This structure, often referred to as "block one," includes four modules, two provided by the U.S. and one each by Japan and the European Space Agency, mounted at the center of a truss structure with solar power capture devices on each end. A servicing facility with a remote manipulator arm, developed by Canada, will also be attached to the structure. The cost estimate of $3.5 billion by 1993 includes $500 million for development of a crew emergency rescue vehicle that is not yet formally part of the program. Congressional Budget Office, *The NASA Program in the 1990s and Beyond*, pp. 25-29.

15. For a discussion of resource allocation and valuation problems attendant to a cost benefit analysis of the civilian space program see, David H. Moore, "Resource Allocation and the Civilian Space Program," presented at the Association for Public Policy Analysis and Management, Bethesda, Maryland, October 31, 1987 (unpublished).

16. These operating costs when most broadly defined include a capital charge that may include the cost of money and depreciation of capital assets. For a discussion of the concept of a capital charge and its application to the shuttle system, see Congressional Budget Office, *Pricing Options for the Space Shuttle*, pp. 15-19.

16. General Accounting Office, *Cost, Schedule, and Performance of NASA's Galileo Mission to Jupiter*, May 1988, p. 11, and *Status of the Hubble Space Telescope Program*, May 1988, p. 18.

18. Congressional Budget Office, *The NASA Budget in the 1990s and Beyond*, pp. 35-38.

19. National Research Council, *Space Technology to Meet Future Needs* (Washington D.C.: National Academy Press, 1987), pp. 1-4.

20. Michael A. Toman and Molly K. Macauley, "Space Transportation Policy: Commercial Policies and International Competition" in *Economics and Technology in U.S. Space Policy*,

32

Molly K. Macauley, ed. (Washington, D.C.: Resources for the Future, 1986), pp. 201-205.

21. Congressional Budget Office, *The NASA Program in the 1990s and Beyond*, pp. 51-54.

Chapter 2

BARNSTORMING IN SPACE: THE RISE AND FALL
OF THE ROMANTIC ERA OF SPACEFLIGHT, 1957-1986

Alex Roland

So thoroughly had the present prosperity persuaded the
citizens that nothing could withstand them, and that they
could achieve what was possible and impracticable alike,
with means ample or inadequate it mattered not. The
secret of this was their general extraordinary success,
which made them confuse their strength with their hopes.

Thucydides
The Peloponnesian War

Across the seamless web of history, historians stitch seams.
Not to distort the record, or to mislead the reader, but to make
sense out of chaos. History is a never-ending Bayeux tapestry,
interweaving lives and deaths that overlap one another and shape
one another. Any story lifted from it must begin and end
somewhere. Choosing the limits of a historical tale is part of the
historian's responsibility. It is a way of organizing knowledge,
making it comprehensible and discrete.

The eras historians define become the benchmarks of our
historical understanding, the frames in which we come to see and
thus comprehend our past. Renaissance humanists, for example,
gave us the notion of the Dark Ages because they saw themselves
as standing on a cultural plateau comparable to that of Rome at
its height. Between their achievement and Rome's they viewed a
cultural chasm into which Western society had fallen for a
millennium. The term dark ages was exaggerated and misleading,
but it has nonetheless shaped our historical consciousness for five

hundred years. The seams between historical periods may be dramatic and instantaneous, or they may be subtle and invisible. The French Revolution, for example, separates the early modern era from the modern era with a violent and blood-red stitch. The transition from the classical world to the middle ages was stretched out over the slow and painful decline and fall of the Roman Empire. Historians choose their thread and their stitch to match the circumstances they envision.

The most difficult seams to discern are those that haven't been invented yet. If the nuclear age began in 1945, when did it or will it end? When did we pass into the post-industrial age? When did the electronic age begin? Is the Cold War over? We can guess at these eras, but only time will confirm which stitches hold, which are rent. So too with attempts to define the space age. In the wake of the Apollo 11 mission, Arthur Schlesinger, Jr., said that when historians look back on the twentieth century they will recall it above all else as the time when man began the exploration of space. This is more cautious than Richard Nixon's hyperbolic assertion that the eight days of that mission marked "the greatest week in the history of mankind since the Creation," but it is hardly the kind of detached judgment one might expect of a historian.[1] If the space age endures as a useful historical concept, it will need to be developed with more perspective than Professor Schlesinger was able to bring to it in the first flush of the Apollo achievement. Surely we still view the space age as a useful historical concept, but it is not as clear as it seemed in 1969 that the moon landing was the defining event.

I propose that we are now between the first and second stages of the space age. The first stage clearly began with Sputnik, and, as Professor Schlesinger hypothesized, it was focused on man's initial departure from planet earth. The end, however, was not the moon landing but the Challenger accident. From 1957 until 1986, the world went through what I call the romantic era of spaceflight, characterized by a succession of dramatic manned space spectaculars in earth orbit and cislunar space. The nature of the second period is as yet unclear, but it is likely to be much different. Equally unclear is whether Challenger will mark a dramatic transition comparable to the French Revolution or whether the romantic era of spaceflight will pass slowly and perhaps painfully into some more advanced stage. In either event, the transition is under way.

A romantic first stage in human developments is not an unfamiliar phenomenon, especially when the developments surround technological revolutions. Sputnik's ability to escape the surface of the earth shocked the human imagination; when Yuri Gagarin followed in 1961, the effect was even more profound. Through technological ingenuity, modern man had separated his generation from all others that went before, setting off flights of imagination of the kind that transported Professor Schlesinger. These events created what the historian Carl Becker called a new "climate of opinion." Seventeenth century in origin, the term refers to those "instinctively held preconceptions in the broad sense, that *Weltanshaung* or world pattern."[2] When fostered by technological revolutions like Sputnik or manned spaceflight, new climates of opinion often take the form of romantic enthusiasms for a utopian future that seems ordained by the new technology, a kind of manifest destiny of the machine that seems just as sure and just as important to the initiate as religious belief is to the faithful.

Similar enthusiasm greeted the introduction of steam power in the nineteenth century, making of James Watt a national and international hero and transforming the age's view of its future. Electricity had a similar effect when it was finally reduced to human service at the hands of another international hero, Thomas Edison. Henry Adams captured some of this wonderment surrounding these two achievements when he compared the "silent and infinite force" of the dynamos at the Great Exposition of 1900 with the moral force that "early Christians felt [for] the Cross" and that medieval pilgrims and peasants felt for the Virgin Mary in her cathedral at Chartres.[3] The dynamo and the virgin, he came to believe, were symbols and drivers of their respective ages. Closer to our own time, nuclear power seemed to open up boundless opportunities for those who understood its potential, leading Atomic Energy Commission Chairman Lewis Strauss to predict that electricity would soon be "too cheap to meter."[4] The "green revolution" of the following decade sparked equally utopian visions of a world without hunger.[5] Indeed, utopianism has become one of the concomitants of technological breakthroughs. Nuclear power and the new agricultural technology have transformed our world forever, but not in the way the enthusiasts first envisioned. Star Wars and the National Aerospace Plane are just as likely to fall short of the hyperbolic rhetoric surrounding their introduction.[6]

The nearest parallel to the romantic era of spaceflight came in the barnstorming era of aviation.[7] Sputnik may be equated with the first flight of the Wright brothers in 1903, though of course the latter received far less public exposure. The Russian and American manned flights of 1961 parallel in many ways the flights of Wilbur Wright in Paris and Orville Wright in Washington in 1908, which Charles Gibbs-Smith came to call the *annus mirabilis* of aviation, the year in which all the world came to recognize the true nature and the implications of the Wrights' achievement.[8] Of course the moon landing of 1969 bears comparison with Lindbergh's 1927 crossing of the Atlantic, events watched and heralded around the world and making international heroes out of the Lone Eagle on the one hand and Neil Armstrong and his colleagues on the other. Through most of these adventures, the flyers themselves were almost as important in the public imagination as the technologies that carried them aloft. Eddie Richenbacher, Wiley Post, and Amelia Earhart come as quickly to mind as Yuri Gagarin, John Glenn, and Sally Ride.[9]

The parallels between early aviation and spaceflight transcend the public persona of the flyers. Both technologies had immediately apparent civilian and military potentials, but in neither case was it entirely clear how they would be exploited.[10] On the military side reconnaissance was seen as the first and most important role. Aircraft were in fact designed and used primarily for that purpose in World War I, where it was discovered that air superiority, close air support, and even strategic bombing held out still greater potential. So too has the military use of space been given over primarily to reconnaissance so far, though communications has moved increasingly to the forefront and Star Wars looms on the horizon.

Civilian uses of aviation were slower to develop, mail delivery giving way to passenger travel and finally large-scale freight transportation only well after the early romantic era was over; in spite of valiant early attempts, aerial photography and weather forecasting played only peripheral roles. In space, communications and scientific research have dominated civilian exploitation, with weather and earth resources playing lesser roles. Civilian aviation required large public subsidies, provided directly to national airlines in most countries and indirectly through research support and the Department of Commerce in the United States. So too in space, where scientific research has been subsidized almost entirely by the federal government, and the one commercial success so far, the communications satellite, has proceeded through a revolutionary public/private venture, COMSAT. Other civilian activities in space have been paid for almost entirely at public expense.

The closest parallel between the romantic era of aviation and the romantic era of spaceflight came in what historian Joseph Corn has called "the winged gospel," the almost religious enthusiasm for the new technology that flourished in the United States in the early twentieth century.[11] A similar enthusiasm for manned spaceflight, a climate of opinion, holds sway over many Americans today. Buffs in the 1920s fastened on aviation firsts, like the first plane to commute from home to office, and my personal favorite, the first cat to fly the English Channel.[12] These may be compared with our recent infatuation with the first man in space, the first extra-vehicular activity, the first woman in space, and the first golf shot on the moon. Talk of a "space age" and "space-age technology" is reminiscent of earlier visions of an "aerial age," a "true" or "real" air age, a "new epoch," and a "mighty era" that promised a "great new future of the world."[13] It was confidently predicted in the 1920s that explorers would henceforth make their discoveries from the air, that real estate agents would show property from on high, that travelling salesmen would use their planes as mobile showrooms, and that hunters would chase birds in flight.[14] Today we hear analogous prophecies of cheap manufacturing in space, resorts in Earth orbit, and mail delivery by rocket. The most familiar theme of the winged gospel was "a plane in every garage," comparable to the myth of a Space Shuttle that "everyman" could fly.[15] William Randolph Hearst's brilliant and cynical Junior Birdmen of America compares sadly with today's spacecamps, which build a political constituency by promising wide-eyed children an impossible future.[16]

One characteristic of the aviation visionaries of the 1920s is that they based their prophecies on the history that they knew. Alexander Graham Bell predicted in 1909 that the "aerial motor car" was just around the corner, displaying not unfettered vision but the most parochial myopia.[17] As is often true of such utopianism, which is always a climate of opinion unto itself, it was both an exaggeration and an underestimation of what came to pass. The early visionaries failed to anticipate the high-speed commercial airliners that have shrunken the world to a commuting ground for jet setters and businessmen. Instead they took their own world of the emerging automobile and superimposed the airplane upon it.

So too have the visionaries of the early space age imagined futures that are mere extrapolations of our experience with aviation. On the one hand they have been moved to wildly unrealistic predictions of the volume and facility of spaceflight, building the Apollo launch facilities, for example, to handle fifty Saturn launches a year[18] and predicating Shuttle operations on a similar estimate of fifty launches annually.[19] As in the barnstorming days of aviation, the adventure of people flying as an end in itself has captured the imagination of the enthusiasts and shaped the future they foresee. The Shuttle was designed in part to recreate the experience of flight for "everyman," either by allowing earthbound citizens to fly vicariously with the aviator or astronaut or to actually take them along for a joyride themselves.[20] It was for this that we have been subjected to the spectacle of the senator in space, the congressman in space, the Saudi prince in space, and finally the teacher in space. The tragedy of that last adventure spared us the journalist in space, proceeding inexorably to the man-in-the-street in space. About these adventures hung the same carnival atmosphere that greeted the barnstormers of the 1920s, who flew into Backwater township to take Aunt Hazel up for her first and usually last spin among the clouds. The real future of aviation, however, lay elsewhere. It was designed not at the air races or the fair ground but in the government research laboratories and the aircraft manufacturing plants. It was created not by barnstormers and recordbreakers -- though they played their part -- but by the engineers and businessmen and soldiers who transformed the airplane from a toy and a curiosity into a practical vehicle for transportation and national security.[21] The "airframe revolution" of the early 1930s which gave us the DC-3 transformed the airplane from circus horse into workhorse.[22] War and commerce shaped the future of aviation. So too will they shape the future of spaceflight.

The analogy between barnstorming and the romantic era of spaceflight should not be pushed too far, if only because spaceflight has not yet emerged from its romantic phase. Neither war nor commerce has yet provided the necessary spur to rational exploitation of space. Though Star Wars looms on the horizon, it is yet unclear when or if it will come to pass. Reconnaissance has historically been the most important military use of space,[23] and though this undertaking has expanded the military space budget to more than twice NASA's[24] it does not of itself promise to support the order-of-magnitude increase in activity that would be necessary to expand spaceflight in the way that military aviation grew in the middle of the twentieth century. On the civilian side, commercial activities seem to have reached a plateau beyond which they are not likely to advance in the current technological dispensation. Communications satellites remain an important commercial technology, but their future growth is more likely to be qualitative than quantitative. Failing a major national commitment to large-scale use of solar power collection in space, it seems unlikely that any commercial venture in space is going to greatly increase the development of "infrastructure" there.[25]

Surely weather satellites and earth resources satellites will continue their incremental development, but neither seems likely to be a major commercial success. Talk of manufacturing in space, which has been going on for a quarter century or more, is still just that -- talk.

How, then, and when might the transformation to the second era of spaceflight be completed? Again, the answer is unclear. But it is apparent that the change is being delayed by our current national policies. The institutional home of our civilian space program is locked into a climate of opinion bred of Sputnik, Gagarin, and Apollo. It is intent upon extending the romantic era of spaceflight -- indeed upon building our whole future in space around a program of barnstorming. We are in a state of suspended adolescence, deferring mature exploitation of space in a childish infatuation with circus.

The origins of this anachronism are in the Apollo program. When Thomas O. Paine succeeded James E. Webb as administrator of NASA in 1969 he found the space agency in a paradoxical situation. Just months before the first moon landing, on the eve of one of the greatest technological triumphs of all time, NASA was experiencing budget cuts. In fact the agency's budget had been falling steadily since 1965, the midpoint of the Apollo undertaking.[26] Instead of the ambitious and exciting adventure in space that Apollo had seemed to promise, NASA faced a diminished and cloudy future. The second half of the 1960s had brought the United States a debilitating war abroad, domestic unrest, rioting in major cities, environmental crisis, and spectacular shortfalls in the federal budget. President Johnson had turned a deaf ear to proposals for an ambitious follow-on program to Apollo and Congress had called with increasing emphasis for practical payoffs on the $25 billion dollars it had already invested in getting to the moon.[27] Congressman Joseph E. Karth, Chairman of the Space Science and Applications Subcommittee predicted in September 1969 that "the pressure on Congress to reduce the space budget still further will increase unless the orientation of NASA is based less on space spectaculars and more on the production of tangible and economic benefits."[28] The success that awaited NASA in the summer of 1969 was to be rewarded with retrenchment.

Administrator Paine was not about to oversee the dismantling of the Apollo team. He was a space enthusiast of the first order, driven like many of his colleagues in NASA to pursue what they perceived as man's destiny in the heavens. If the country faced a succession of demoralizing crises in the late 1960s, then it was all the more in need of Apollo, a spectacular national success in a decade gone sour. Richard Nixon, an old friend of the space program, was in the White House and no doubt open to a proposal that might move beyond the moon mission which was, after all, the creature of his former nemesis John Kennedy. In short, 1969 presented an opportunity for Paine and NASA to map out a new future for the agency, one more exciting than the politicians were able to see from the well of gloom into which they had fallen.

Paine quickly pressed President Nixon for a major new initiative in space. Nixon hesitated, appointing instead a Space Task Group to study the problem under the direction of his vice president, Spiro Agnew. In September 1969, two months after the first Apollo landing, the STG came in with its report.[29] It recommended Mars and a Space Station; the main purpose of the Space Station was to go to Mars. The report called for a balanced program that included space science and applications, but the overall pace and direction of the agency's agenda was tied to a barnstorming tour of the Red Planet.

The first choice of the Task Group was a commitment then and there to a manned Mars mission. Like Apollo, on which it was clearly modeled, this mission would send men to Mars as an end in itself.

Space science played a role, but the most important goal was to develop "new challenges for man in space."[30] (Read barrel rolls and Immelmann turns in the shadow of Phobos.) If a Mars landing in the early 1980s was too ambitious, the Task Group continued, the country could commit itself to a less expensive, more slowly paced program that would end up on Mars in the second half of the 1980s. Failing those two options, the President could simply opt for a Space Station and a Shuttle to ferry crew and supplies to and from the Station. The principal rationale for a Space Station since the nineteenth century had been as a way-Station to the planets, so even this third option supported the same goal.[31]

The Space Task Group echoed the NASA philosophy of the 1960s. It made manned spaceflight an end in itself and it proposed a series of "logical steps" as the centerpiece of the civilian space program in the decades to come. Beginning with Neil Armstrong's "one small step for [a] man, one giant leap for mankind," each successive step was a manned adventure, eschewing incremental advance in favor of quantum leaps in technological capability and developmental goals. Apollo had demonstrated that we could do anything we set our minds to. All that was left was to lay out the agenda and get to work. The enterprise was simply too important and too exciting to be left to the timid and cautious.

The mentality that was driving this proposal appeared most clearly in a planning conference held the following June at the NASA research facility on Wallops Island, Virginia.[32] There Paine called together his top executives for a brainstorming session on the future of "Spaceship NASA." Wernher von Braun lamented before his colleagues the "cruise ship model of human existence" then gripping the country, an apparent reference to building a launch vehicle like the Saturn and then using it for nothing more exciting than the Skylab Space Station. Paine proposed instead "fighting ships . . . both naval and buccaneering as the non-cruise ship nautical model for NASA."[33] He asked his colleagues to "consider NASA as "Nelson's 'Band of Brothers' -- Sea Rovers" of "swashbuckling buccaneer courage" who would "stake out and create powerful outposts of stability, sanity and real future value for mankind in the new uncharted seas of space and global technology." Though the conferees identified some useful and practical technological objectives, such as new methods of food synthesis and improved engines and generators, it is nonetheless clear that they were in the throes of a romantic enthusiasm of Byronic proportions, a climate of opinion that left them deaf and blind to alternative futures in space. Men were going to sail on what President Kennedy called "this new sea;"[34] nothing else would do. Their vision of the future of spaceflight and how to achieve it made the modest goals of the barnstormers pale by comparison.[35]

The wonder is not so much that NASA executives should think in such terms in 1970; in the intoxicating wake of the first moon landing even sober observers like Arthur Schlesinger, Jr., were given to hyperbole and flights of imagination. What is remarkable is that the agenda laid out in that first flush of enthusiasm has continued to hold sway over NASA through all the succeeding years. The agency is still committed to the succession of "next logical steps" envisioned in the Space Task Group report of 1969.[36] It settled for the Shuttle as the major undertaking of the 1970s, characterizing it as part of a space transportation system designed to support a Space Station, which was in turn a way Station to Mars. When the Shuttle became "fully operational" after its fourth flight in 1982, NASA immediately pressed the Reagan administration to authorize the "next logical step," the Station,[37] which the President approved in his State of the Union Address in 1984.[38] Now, with the Station hardly beyond the design stage,

NASA is already arguing about whether to go back to the moon next or proceed directly to Mars.[39]

The problem with this agenda is that it is driven by romance not practicality. There are many worthwhile things to do in space; sending people there is one of the most expensive and least productive. It perhaps provides psychic income to those who thrill to such adventures, but the practical returns are far more difficult to identify. Like Charles Lindbergh's flight across the Atlantic or Amelia Earhart's failed attempt to circumnavigate the earth, these flights are primarily stunts to show that we can do them. After the moon landings, few people doubt that we are capable of sending men to Mars. If it were free, it would no doubt be worth doing. But in fact it and the other "logical steps" NASA has been pursuing for almost twenty years are extremely dangerous and ruinously expensive.

It costs ten times as much to conduct a space mission with people as it does with automated spacecraft.[40] The reason is simple. On a manned spaceflight you not only have to carry the extra weight of the crew but also the food, water, medicine, oxygen, and life-support equipment on which their survival depends. Additionally, and more importantly, you have to "man-rate" the spacecraft, i.e., build in redundant features, maintain rigid quality control on the manufacture of all components, and ensure reliability to levels that would be simply impractical on an unmanned vehicle. Just the documentation for a manned spaceflight is an administrative and financial burden that raises costs by an order of magnitude. George Low, the late head of manned spaceflight, Deputy Administrator of NASA, and stalwart defender of man in space once told a colleague that "it had cost 10 times as much to prepare a magnetometer for the Apollo project as it had to prepare a similar one for an unmanned project."[41]

Over the past quarter century, two-thirds of our space dollars have been invested in manned spaceflight, with little to show for the investment save circus.[42] By and large it has been wonderful circus, just as the barnstorming was, but hardly more productive. The major achievement of the astronauts and cosmonauts to date is the accumulation of physiological data to determine their ability to survive long periods in space, should we ever find a reason for sending them there. The real payoff in space -- the work of the communications satellites, the weather and earth resources satellites, the scientific probes -- has been funded by the remaining one third of the civilian space budget.

NASA offers two good reasons for its continuing concentration on manned spaceflight; behind them lurk the two real reasons. The first good reason is the man with a screwdriver. We need people on our spacecraft, so the argument goes, to respond to the unexpected. People are versatile and adaptive; machines are programmed and inflexible. Skylab is the ultimate example.

Launched unmanned on 14 May 1973, Skylab suffered serious damage on ascent and arrived in orbit with part of its meteoroid shield torn away, one of its two solar wings lost, and the other jammed shut.[43] Underpowered and overexposed to sunlight, the craft heated up to uninhabitable levels and threatened to preclude the manned visits that were to follow. The first visit, launched just eleven days later, turned into a rescue mission of high drama and heroic performance, both by the astronauts in orbit and the ground crews that designed and directed the rescue. The astronauts deployed the remaining solar wing and placed a jury-rigged cover over the exposed portion of the fuselage; internal temperatures fell and power rose to levels adequate for operation of the spacecraft and its equipment. A disastrous accident had been turned into an exciting salvage and a new legend had been added to the lore of manned spaceflight. The resourcefulness and versatility of the astronauts *in situ* had saved the mission and demonstrated the value of men in space.

The other good reason for men in space is that manned spaceflight has become a highly visible and widely appreciated measure of technological achievement in the Cold War race for prestige. The National Aeronautics and Space Act of 1958 specifically enjoins NASA to make the United States "a leader" in space activity; surely Congress wanted to race the Russians in space when it adopted that legislation.[44] This was the primary motive driving the Apollo program at the outset,[45] but not even that conclusive victory seems to have settled the issue. The Soviet Union continues to support a large, highly publicized manned program, capturing in the years since Skylab most of the records for achievement and endurance in orbit. Though no outsider can claim to discern with confidence Soviet motives, it seems clear that the Russians still believe that they reap a significant harvest of international prestige from their manned spaceflight accomplishments. Secretary General Gorbachev's invitation to President Reagan for the United States to join the Soviet Union in a manned mission to Mars is in keeping with the same spirit that moved the Russians into the Apollo-Soyuz Test Project of 1975, to pose as a technological equal of the United States by matching their manned spaceflight achievements and participating with them in joint ventures.[46] Why the U.S. feels compelled to keep running the same race over is less clear, but we seem nonetheless committed to matching the Russians Space Station for Space Station indefinitely.

Both of these arguments are compelling; both are seriously flawed. First of all, the man with a screwdriver usually costs more than he is worth, in part because he isn't worth all that much. For every Skylab mission that can be cited, there are a dozen manned missions where the people on board did not begin to pay their way in any practical sense. Far from being an asset on most space missions, astronauts are a liability. Not only does the mission have to sustain the extra weight and bulk of them and their life support mechanisms, it also has to follow a flight plan dictated primarily by the safety of the crew. It cannot go too far from Earth, as the Voyager spacecraft have. It cannot travel in harm's way, as Pioneer 10 did when it passed through the asteroid belt between Mars and Jupiter or when it exposed itself to the full strength of Jupiter's radiation fields, 10,000 times more intense than the Earth's Van Allen belts. It cannot shut down its systems in flight to save power, as most of our unmanned spacecraft do on long missions. Nor can it completely change its mission profile as Voyager 2 did on the way to the outer planets.[47] Both Voyager spacecraft are likely to be still transmitting to us in the 21st century from nine billion miles away; manned spaceflights are pedestrian by comparison.

Nor is the Skylab mission all that persuasive as a model for the utility of manned spaceflight. After all, the crew was able to repair the craft only because it could design the rescue on earth and load up with the proper equipment before launch. An astronaut on the Martian surface with the wrong screwdriver would be just as useless as a computer in the same position. If the astronaut took all the right tools, then someone on earth had anticipated all the problems; in which case you don't need the astronaut in the first place. The real model for human versatility in space is the Apollo 13 mission, in which the flight directors in Houston designed and effected the rescue. The astronauts simply went along for the ride, though their presence necessitated the rescue in the first place. Had it been an automated flight, the spacecraft, which was no longer able to perform its mission, would simply have been abandoned. This is the way most of our missions run, with controllers on earth guiding and reprogramming our automated flights to adapt to new and unforeseen circumstances. The human element is important, but it doesn't have to be *in situ*.

The Viking missions to Mars, the most expensive space science undertaking of the 1970s and perhaps the most technically sweet experiment in the history of spaceflight, revealed more clearly than any other enterprise the power of American space technology and the capabilities of remotely controlled vehicles. In 1975 the United States launched two spacecraft from earth on the 500-million-mile missions to Mars.[48] Viking 1 arrived on 20 July 1976 and began to survey the Martian surface. Finding the original landing site unsatisfactory, it searched about for two weeks. When it had identified a suitable site, it detached a lander which flew to the surface and soft-landed. Deploying an array of instruments and sensors, the lander began to survey the Martian environment. Most importantly, perhaps, it sampled the soil in its vicinity and tested the material in an on-board laboratory, attempting to answer the fundamental question of the mission: was there, or had there ever been, life on Mars? The results were finally inconclusive, but they gave little encouragement to those who believed that the planet is or was capable of supporting life.

Viking 2 arrived on 3 September 1976. It too orbited the planet and successfully dispatched its lander to the surface, setting down at another site believed conducive to life. The results of its tests were similarly indeterminate. The two failures together fed the growing pessimism about the possibility of life on Mars.

If these spacecraft did not finally resolve the issue of life on the Red Planet, they nonetheless provided a model for how to operate in space. The spacecraft, indeed the whole mission, were designed by men and women who programed the vehicles to do what they would do if they were on the Martian surface or in Martian orbit. They imagined in advance what life would be like if it existed on Mars and how you would test for traces of it, and they designed their experiments accordingly. Just as astronauts would take certain equipment and supplies if they were going to Mars themselves, based on their expectations of what they would find there, so too did the scientists and engineers on earth build into the Viking spacecraft the capabilities and characteristics they expected would be needed.

The mission flew two spacecraft to increase the probability that at least one would get through. The project team negotiated in advance all the trade-offs between the desires of the scientists to run experiments and the insistence of the engineers that the spacecraft function properly. The engineers of necessity won the close calls. As it happened both craft worked almost flawlessly and operated well beyond their rated capacities. Through ingenious reprogramming from earth, the expected mission life of the two orbiters was extended from ninety days to almost two years for Orbiter 2 and over four years for Orbiter 1, which sent back data until it finally ran out of fuel on 6 August 1980. Lander 1 sent back data for over six years, until it reportedly ran out of fuel in 1983.[49] These spacecraft did everything that was expected of them and more. If they failed to find life on Mars it was because there is no life there to find or people here on earth asked the wrong questions or put them in the wrong place. It is difficult to see how humans on the expedition might have done more or better. In fact humans on earth controlled the spacecraft throughout their flights and directed their activities once they had landed.[50]

The Viking mission to Mars cost about $1 billion in 1975 dollars, a very large sum by space science standards but a pittance on the scale of manned spaceflight. The Apollo program had cost $25 billion in 1960s dollars just to go to the moon. A manned Mars mission would have cost at least several times as much. It would have brought back some Martian samples for study here on earth, but it is possible to build machines to do that, as the Russians did with their Lunar moon vehicle in the 1960s. The Viking mission to Mars demonstrates with compelling clarity the most fundamental weakness of manned spaceflight: any specific mission we can identify to conduct in space we can build a machine to do. And we can do it more quickly, more safely, and at a fraction of the cost of sending people up to do it.

The prestige argument for manned spaceflight is less specific than the man-with-a-screwdriver, and for that reason less easy to pin down. There is no doubt that a certain cachet attaches to manned spaceflight and that Apollo returned to the U.S. just what it went after -- the international prestige of being the best in space. It is also clear that at least in the public eye, manned spaceflight is more important than any other space activity in establishing preeminence in space. It is not clear, however, that the country is willing to "pay any price" as President Kennedy put it in 1961 in order to match the Russians, especially now when peace is breaking out all over the world.

Furthermore, the emptiness of manned spaceflight is beginning to catch up with its reputation. Cosmonauts have been around the earth some 32,000 times now and they have virtually nothing to show for it save atrophied muscles and frazzled psyches. Their comings and goings to and from their Space Stations are reported in the press but given little attention. When the Challenger exploded in 1986, the major networks were not covering the launch because the ratings were terrible. Christa McCauliffe was needed on the flight in part to boost public interest in what was becoming a ho-hum performance. The same public indifference even plagued the later Apollo missions, arguably the most exciting space ventures to date. Prestige may well attach to these undertakings, but it is the ability to do it, not the repetition that captures the public imagination. If we are going to have manned flights, we should reserve them for those unusual and demanding missions that might really benefit from human presence; leave the routine flights to the machines. This would entail no loss in international prestige; on the contrary, it might revive international interest. Prestige is an arguably rational goal for manned spaceflight; it is not a good reason for building our whole space program around manned spacecraft and facilities in space.

The real reasons why NASA has built the civilian space program around a succession of manned space spectaculars are seldom discussed in public. First, it has been an article of faith within NASA since the budget cuts of the late 1960s that manned spaceflight sells. NASA and its supporters have been trying for twenty years to recapture the level of funding they enjoyed in the immediate aftermath of the Kennedy commitment to the moon mission. They view that as the appropriate level of national support for this crucial undertaking, and they view all budgets since as something of a cutback. The only way to return to those budget levels, they argue, is for the country to commit itself once more to a major, manned undertaking like Apollo. They made that argument when selling the Shuttle; they made it again in selling the Space Station; and they are making it now in selling a Mars mission as a follow-on to the Station.

This rationale is flawed on two levels. First, it doesn't work. Apollo was a crash program designed to address a unique set of historical circumstances. Five administrations and seven congresses have made it clear that the country is not likely to engage in such an undertaking any time soon, surely not on a regular basis. Rather, the country has supported NASA at a steady-state level. Since 1973 the civilian space budget has been approximately $7.8 billion in constant 1988 dollars; it has not varied more than 10 percent above or below that figure, save for the extra funding provided in the aftermath of the Challenger accident.[51] President Nixon's staff explicitly told NASA when it was negotiating for the Shuttle that it could expect a steady-state budget over the term of his presidency. Other administrations have tacitly told NASA the same thing, and Congress has gone along. Grandiose proposals like the early shuttle configurations and the early Space Station plans only get pared down to bargain basement versions then struggle along trying to reach completion under the existing budget ceiling. The result is scaled-down, stretched-out, and unsatisfactory manned projects and the squeezing of other NASA programs to try to keep the spectaculars alive. We watched this all through Shuttle development and that history is now repeating itself with the Station.

The rationale fails on yet another level because NASA has made of it a self-fulfilling prophecy. Believing that only manned spaceflight sells before Congress and the public, it has never given proper exposure to its unmanned programs. NASA's truly spectacular achievements in space science, earth resources monitoring, geodesy, and weather analysis have gone comparatively unnoticed. Public relations at NASA is built around astronauts, in part because the public shows the greatest interest in them, but in part also because NASA has always put them out front. If NASA invested as much effort in selling its unmanned programs, it would have a wider and more solid base of support than it does now.

But the final, real reason that NASA has built the civilian space program around a succession of manned space spectaculars is a climate of opinion. The agency continues in the grip of an emotional enthusiasm for the spectacle of manned spaceflight itself. NASA is filled with space enthusiasts, sharing with Tom Paine an enthusiasm and zeal for peopling the universe that approaches a religious faith. Man's destiny is in the stars, they believe, and it is their mission to put him there. Accepting anything less would be an abomination of human nature and a compromise with destiny. They consider themselves to be, as Paine put it on Wallops Island, the keepers of the "boldest and most visionary goals," entrusted with "moving the planet into a better 21st century." They have no conception of why man should go into space, nor what he will do once there, but they are determined that he must go nonetheless.

This is the "winged gospel" of the barnstormers translated into the late twentieth century. In it are the seeds of our future. In it also is much silly fluff, romantic nonsense that will remain science fiction long after other, unimagined avenues in space are opened up and explored. Distinguishing between the fact and fiction entails hard calculations about cost effectiveness and the utility of what we are trying to accomplish in space. For only when the activity starts paying off on earth will it attract the funding necessary to realize its full potential. The issues of war and peace that are likely to provide that incentive are now being clouded by our romantic enthusiasms. It is time to grow up and get on with the business of space exploration and exploitation.

NOTES

1. Public Papers of the Presidents of the United States, Richard M. Nixon, 1969 (Washington, D.C.: General Services Administration, 1971), p. 542.

2. Carl Becker, *The Heavenly City of the Eighteenth-century Philosophes* (New London: Yale University Press, 1932), p. 5.

3. Henry Adams, *The Education of Henry Adams: An Autobiography* (New York: Houghton-Mifflin, 1988), p. 380.

4. Lewis Straus speech of 16 September 1954, quoted in Daniel Ford, *The Cult of the Atom: The Secret Papers of the Atomic Energy Commission* (New York: Simon and Schuster, 1982), p. 50.

5. Clifton R. Wharton, Jr., "The Green Revolution: Cornucopia or Pandora's Box?" *Foreign Affairs* 47, 1969: 464-76.

6. Military leaders have said the aerospace plane could reduce launch costs by 99%, the same kind of claim that was made for the shuttle. See Stephen W. Korthals-Altes, "Will the Aerospace Plane work?" *Technology Review* 43, January 1987.

7. The best survey of American aviation history is Roger Bilstein, *Flight in America, 1900-1983: From the Wrights to the Astronauts* (Baltimore: The Johns Hopkins University Press, 1984). Bilstein concentrates on the developments that were to produce real advances in aviation; consequently he devotes little attention to the barnstormers. Note, however, his treatment of "The Adventurers," pp. 83-85, and his observation that "in headlines and crowds, the men and women who flew the planes received the sort of acclaim granted to astronauts a generation later." A fuller treatment of the romantic era of aviation is C.R. Roseberry, *The Challenging Skies: The Colorful Story of Aviation's Most Exciting Years, 1919-1939* (Garden City, N.Y.: Doubleday, 1966), esp. chap. 4, "The Rollicking Barnstormers."

8. Charles H. Gibbs-Smith, *The Aeroplane: A Historical Survey of Its Origins and Development* (London: Science Museum, 1960), p. 59.

9. Chuck Yeager did not become a household word until Tom Wolfe popularized him as the ultimate holder of the right stuff. Tom Wolfe, *The Right Stuff* (New York: Farar, Straus, Giroux, 1979).

10. For military aviation, Michael Sherry uses the term "the age of fantasy," similar in many ways to what I mean by the romantic era of spaceflight. See his *The Rise of American Air Power: The Creation of Armageddon* (New Haven: Yale University Press, 1987), chap. 1.

11. Joseph J. Corn, *The Winged Gospel: America's Romance with Aviation, 1900-1950* (New York: Oxford University Press, 1983).

12. *Ibid.*, p. 10.

13. *Ibid.*, p. 32.

14. *Ibid.*, pp. 32-33.

15. *Ibid.*, chap. 5.

16. *Ibid.*, chap. 6.

17. *Ibid.*, p. 32.

18. Charles D. Benson and William Barnaby Faherty, *Moonport: A History of Apollo Launch Facilities and Operations* (Washington, D.C.: NASA SP-4204, NASA, 1978), p. 529.

19. George E. Mueller, "The New Future for Manned Spacecraft Developments," *Astronautics and Aeronautics* 28, March 1969.

20. See Tom Wolfe, "Everyman vs. Astropower," *Newsweek*, February 10, 1986: 40.

21. Sherry, *The Rise of American Airpower*, chap. 1.

22. Bilstein, *Flight in America*, pp. 85-96. See also John B. Rae, *Climb to Greatness: The American Aircraft Industry, 1920-1960* (Cambridge: MIT Press, 1968).

23. In a famous gaffe in 1967, Lyndon Johnson revealed that the $35-40 billion the United States had then spent on space was worth, in his opinion, ten times that much because the reconnaissance satellites had revealed information about Soviet military power that kept us from taking unnecessary military steps of our own. Chalmers M. Roberts, *The Nuclear Years* (New York: Preager, 1971), p. 87.

24. The avalanche of funding for Apollo that began in fiscal year 1961 raised NASA's budget above the level of military spending on space in that year. NASA's budget remained above the military space budget until fiscal year 1982; four years later it was twice NASA's. *Aeronautics and Space Report of the President, 1987*, appendix E.

25. On the concept of infrastructure in space, see Office of Technology Assessment, *Civilian Space Stations and the U.S. Future in Space* (Washington, D.C.: OTA, 1984).

26. It was $5,137.6 million in 1965, $3,822 million in 1969. This represented a drop of 26% in actual dollars and 34% in constant dollars. *Ibid.*

27. W. Henry Lambright, *Presidential Management of Science and Technology: The Johnson Presidency* (Austin: University of Texas Press, 1985), pp. 141-51.

28. Quoted in Ken Hechler, *The Endless Space Frontier: A History of the House Committee on Science and Astronautics*, 1959-1978, abr. by Albert E. Eastman, AAS History Series, Vol. 4 (San Diego, CA: American Astronautical Society, 1982), p. 293.

29. *The Post-Apollo Program: Directions for the Future, Space Task Group Report to the President* (Washington, September 1969).

30. *Ibid.*, p. 5.

31. Barton D. Hacker, "And Rest As on a Natural Station: From Space Station to Orbital Operations in Space Travel Thought, 1895-1951," unpublished paper [1972], NASA History Office Archives, Washington, D.C.

32. Memorandum, NASA Deputy Associate Administrator to Program Associate Administrators, on "Principal Wallops Island Action Items," undated, in von Braun Library/Archive, A-SRC, Huntsville, AL. The file folder indicates that the meeting was 11-14 June 1970.

33. Paine is a student of naval history, with a large personal library and at least one publication in the field: *Submarining: Three Thousand Books and Articles* (Santa Barbara, CA: General Electric Co.-TEMPO, Center for Advanced Studies, [1971]).

34. *Public Papers of the Presidents of the United States, John F. Kennedy, 1962* (Washington, D.C.: General Services Administration, 1963), p. 669.

35. The swashbuckling episode was first made public by Homer Newell in his *Beyond the Atmosphere: Early Years of Space Science* (Washington, D.C.: NASA SP-4211; NASA, 1980), p. 288. Newell notes that Paine later questioned the appropriateness of the term.

36. "The Next Logical Step," NASA Brochure (Washington, D.C.: NASA, no date)

37. James M. Beggs to Edwin Meese, III, May 21, 1982; copy in the possession of the author.

38. "The State of the Union," January 25, 1984, *Weekly Compilation of Presidential Documents* 20, (January 30, 1984): 84.

39. See, for example, the Ride report and the swirl of controversy that surrounded it. *Leadership and America's Future in Space, A Report to the Administrator* (Washington, D.C.: NASA, August 1987).

40. Newell, *Beyond the Atmosphere*, pp. 162-63.

41. *Ibid.*, p. 390.

42. Hans Mark and Arnold Levine, *The Management of Research Institutions: A Look at Government Laboratories* (Washington, D.C.: NASA SP-481, NASA, 1984). One recent researcher put the figure even higher, at 80%; see T.A. Heppenheimer, "Son of Space Station," *Discover*, (July 1988): p. 64.

52

43. W. David Compton and Charles D. Benson, *Living and Working in Space: A History of Skylab* (Washington, D.C: NASA SP-4208, NASA, 1983).

44. Robert L. Rosholt, *An Administrative History of NASA, 1958-1963* (NASA SP-4101, Washington, D.C.: NASA, 1966); Allison Griffith, *The National Aeronautics and Space Act: A Study of the Development of Public Policy* (Washington, D.C.: Public Affairs Press, 1969).

45. Vernon Van Dyke, *Pride and Power: The Rationale of the Space Program* (Urbana: University of Illinois Press, 1964); and John Logsdon, *The Decision To Go To The Moon: Project Apollo and the National Interest* (Chicago: University of Chicago Press, [1970] 1976).

46. Edward Clinton Ezell and Linda Neuman Ezell, *The Partnership: A History of the Apollo-Soyuz Test Project* (NASA SP-4209, Washington, D.C.: NASA, 1978); Walter A. McDougall, *. . . the Heavens and the Earth: A Political History of the Space Age* (New York: Basic Books, 1985).

47. Michael Gold, "Voyager to the Seventh Planet," *Science 86* (May 1986): 32-38.

48. Edward Clinton Ezell and Linda Neuman Ezell, *On Mars: Exploration of the Red Planet, 1958-1978* (NASA SP-4212, Washington, D.C.: NASA, 1984).

49. Edward Hutchings, Jr., "The Autonomous Viking," *Science* 219 (February 18, 1983): 803-808; *New York Times*, May 6, 1983, p. B6; *ibid.*, 23 May 1983, p. A17.

50. The story circulates in the aerospace community that the **Viking 1** lander did not really run out of fuel. Rather an errant signal from a ground controller on Earth pointed the antenna toward the Martian surface, cutting off forever its ability to communicate. If true, this means it was **human error** that terminated this sweetest of automated missions. Of course, an astronaut on Mars with a screwdriver could have righted the antenna, but for the cost of sending and maintaining him there for six years we could send dozens of replacement landers.

51. It is interesting to note, however, that the additional funding received in the wake of the Challenger accident to fix the shuttle program seems to have become permanent, amounting to something like a 25% real increase in the NASA budget over two years in the era of Gramm-Rudman.

Chapter 3

TOWARD A NEW SPACE POLICY

Albert D. Wheelon

FOR A SUCCESSFUL TECHNOLOGY, REALITY MUST TAKE
PRECEDENCE OVER PUBLIC RELATIONS, FOR NATURE CANNOT BE
FOOLED.

R.P. FEYNMAN

PROLOGUE

American space policy is the cumulative result of decisions and
indecisions made by seven successive Presidents. It has been an
increasingly disappointing result. This frustration is a bipartisan
problem. Its solution should be a bipartisan effort.

As we enter the administration of a new president, it is
important to reexamine our national space policy from first
principles. The realization that our present policy is not working
well sets the stage for frank evaluation of where we are going, or
more properly, where we ought to be going.

The first problem is that we do not have a mechanism for
establishing space policy. We do have such a mechanism for
developing defense policy. Each year, the National Security
Council advises the Department of Defense as to what capabilities
the armed forces should be able to provide now and in the future.
For the civil space program, we have only the episodic advocacy
of NASA, the predictable resistance of OMB, and Presidential
resolution or ambivalence. No wide forum exists to debate the
major undertakings that NASA proposes, such as the Space
Station or a manned flight to Mars.

54

The second problem is that NASA's role in the American space program has diminished significantly. The military space program is substantially larger, while satellite communications have flourished under private sponsorship.

Generating a new space policy is thus no easy task. We have been in the space business for only thirty years. We do not have the depth of experience in space that we have in agriculture or transportation. Since we are at the beginning of this new activity, humility is a virtue. We should not hesitate to learn from others, just as we should not hesitate to plot an original course.

REDUNDANCY

Nature is the first great teacher. Human beings have a considerable amount of redundancy. We have two eyes, two ears, two lungs, two kidneys, two legs and two arms. Many people have reason to be grateful for this redundancy. It does not matter if it is the result of Divine design or cruel Darwinian selection: it works.

When the first satellites were designed, this lesson was applied wherever possible. Satellites typically carry two sets of control jets, two separate fuel tanks, and redundant radio equipment. This redundancy was added because satellite repair would be unlikely if not impossible. Some features could not be made redundant: i.e., rocket motors, antennas, bearings and structures. However, the redundancy that could be added has saved countless missions.

The same desire for redundancy is reflected at the next level of integration. Backup spacecraft are provided for virtually all telecommunication systems: Australia, Indonesia, Mexico, Japan, India, Brazil, Canada, Intelsat, Inmarsat, ATT, Western Union, GTE, Hughes, SBS, and the Arab League. Many scientific missions have redundant spacecraft also. Two Vikings landed on Mars and two Voyagers are exploring the outer planets. Military space programs require multiple redundancy since they must plan for intentional problems as well as accidents.

The same push for backup is apparent in ground installations that support space operations. There are two launch pads in Florida for the space shuttle, two for Titan and two for Delta. The Air Force is building a second satellite control facility in Colorado that can back up the primary facility in California.

On an even larger scale, our country is committed to redundancy in its strategic nuclear systems. The Triad philosophy declares that we will maintain three completely independent forces: land based ICBMs, submarine launched missiles, and manned bombers. We do so to ensure that deterrence will be maintained if one -- or even two -- legs of the Triad fail.

The lesson of redundancy is thus written large in nature, in space technology, and in nuclear policy. It should form the basis for any new space policy. This lesson was forgotten in making an exclusive commitment to the Space Shuttle. It has been ignored in recent scientific missions as single spacecraft have replaced redundant programs. It is being ignored in the single large Space Station advocated by NASA.

PRESSURE FOR LARGE SYSTEMS

We should recognize that there are institutional pressures that resist diversity and redundancy. The first pressure is the Economy of Scale argument. This argument states that it is cheaper to add telephone lines to an existing exchange than it is to build a new exchange. It was used for half a century to justify the telephone monopoly. This argument was used for three decades to progressively expand the Air Force Satellite Tracking Facility in California.

The Economy of Scale argument was used to defend a single international system and to argue for larger and larger Intelsat communication satellites. It was argued that it is cheaper to share common spacecraft facilities -- structure, attitude control, and power generation -- than it would be to build several smaller satellites to carry a given number of radio transponders. It was a winsome argument for awhile.

The first problem was that the common facilities became a smaller and smaller part of the cost of a satellite. The radio equipment rapidly began to dominate cost, so the shared facilities became less and less important. Moreover, people began to recognize that initial capital investment was only one measure of space system cost. Replacement cost now looms large in system planning. If one deploys a large single satellite with multiple payloads, its useful life is too often limited by the shortest life of any one of the payloads. Too often, a large multipurpose satellite must be abandoned if only one of its payloads fails or becomes obsolete. The cost of early replacement thus becomes a dominating economic factor.

These issues are now reasonably well understood in space communication companies. After building successively larger satellites for twenty-five years, Intelsat has now ordered a smaller type for its next series. Nonetheless, a general impression persists that large single systems are more cost effective. The Economy of Scale argument is a dangerous guideline for space policy.

A second pressure that leads to large space systems is the pooling of requirements. This happens often in DOD where it is increasingly difficult to start new programs. By recruiting a number of separate missions, each with its own constituency, program managers try to assemble a critical mass of support to get started -- and later avoid cancellation or delay. The problem with this strategy is that one must develop large, multipurpose spacecraft to satisfy all the requirements. Typically, these needs pull in different directions, causing the weight and cost to grow as the design approaches the largest common denominator. That is the story of Milstar.

Most of the DOD spacecraft have become progressively larger and more expensive. Their growth has been limited only by the weight and volume constraints of the space shuttle. Those who are responsible for developing space systems have come to believe that large satellites are the best projects. An institutional preference for large systems has developed in both NASA and DOD. However, this leads to putting more and more eggs into fewer and fewer baskets. This has vulnerability implications for the DOD. For NASA programs, it means a few large spacecraft whose launch and operation must be flawless.

I believe that we are better served if we build smaller spacecraft and provide redundant opportunities for each mission. We did so once. We can do so again if we abandon narrow economic arguments as a basis for space policy.

RESILIENCY

Resiliency and redundancy are complementary virtues. One derives a fair amount of resiliency from having redundant systems. But there is more to it. Resiliency flows from thinking about the consequences of failure as well as success.

Too much of our space policy has been based on optimistic estimates of reliability. Estimates for shuttle reliability were found to be both wrong and misleading by the Rogers Commission. Space is still a very risky business. We will have failures and close calls from time to time. We need to plan what we will do under a wide range of outcomes, both favorable and unfavorable. This is the art of contingency planning.

Resiliency can be enhanced by using unmanned systems, rather than manned systems. The reason is transparent. When a manned system fails, one must be extraordinarily careful about putting it back in operation. The corresponding delay for resuming unmanned operation is about one-third that for manned systems.

Resiliency has another dimension and it is financial. Most space programs overrun their initial contract estimates. In part, this is due to the extraordinary pressure placed on government program managers and contractors alike to be optimistic about costs in the interest of starting new programs. As the programs mature, this shortfall produces acute pain as everyone tries to do an increasingly difficult task with inadequate resources. It is a bad way to develop high technology. Far better that fewer programs begin with adequate financial reserves. Resiliency depends heavily on reserves.

COMMERCIALIZATION

Commercial use of space was pioneered by the United States. NASA played a key role in demonstrating communication satellite technology. The Communication Satellite Act of 1962 created the Comsat Corporation to represent American interests in the new international space telecommunications cooperative. Many other private companies have entered the field. The development of space communication systems to provide both international and domestic service has been an extraordinary success for twenty-five years. It is the first and only successful commercial use of space so far.

The Reagan Administration has sought to replicate this success by commercializing other space activities. These initiatives can be characterized as providing government facilities to private operators who try to make incremental sales on a commercial basis.

The Landsat earth observation system first developed by NASA and then operated by NOAA was "commercialized" by offering the charter and the in-orbit spacecraft to commercial companies on a competitive basis. A contractor team now operates Landsat on funds provided by a government contract for continuing service and the construction of replacement spacecraft. This arrangement is fundamentally no different from the government owned/contractor operated (GOCO) nuclear weapon production facilities.

There was a brief flirtation with "commercializing" the weather satellites, but this was abandoned when it appeared that officials in the Commerce Department were preparing to give the job to Comsat on a negotiated (i.e. non-competitive) basis.

The Department of Transportation took the lead in commercializing expendable launch vehicles. It hoped to make Titan, Delta and Atlas-Centaur available to paying users. NASA was under strong pressure to demonstrate that Shuttle would become an economic success. The key to this success was thought to be heavy loading and rapid flight rates. To achieve these conditions, NASA wanted all satellites flown on Shuttle and pressed to close down the production lines and support facilities for expendable rockets. The loss of Challenger restimulated the commercialization idea and today we have the beginnings of a commercial launch industry.

Commercialization of materials processing in space is another goal of this program. The dream is to make useful -- and possibly unique -- materials in the weightlessness of space. A few successful experiments have been done on Shuttle. Unfortunately, the most promising (electrophoresis) has now been abandoned in favor of genetically engineered drugs here on earth. Hope continues for breakthroughs and this hope provides much of the rationale for a large, manned Space Station.

Commercialization of space is a useful policy component if one recognizes a few important points. It is difficult to commercialize services for which there is no established demand. Telecommunications was a commercial success because an established market existed for that service. Landsat has been difficult to commercialize because the users have been receiving its data for very nominal charges. Weather satellites are even more difficult to make into a business because weather forecasting has always been a government-provided service.

The second obstacle to space commercialization is that most space activities are expensive. The enormous non-recurring cost of a large booster that can place *useful* satellites in space is measured in billions of dollars. Thus far, this charge has been borne in every case by national governments -- both here and abroad. It is unrealistic to imagine that a private company would develop a Titan or Delta on speculation. By contrast, two companies have developed generic communication satellites as commercial ventures more than once and made successes of them.

The moral of the story is this: be careful about proposals to commercialize space activities. Sometimes they work and sometimes they do not -- and cannot.

UNIVERSAL SOLUTIONS

There is a tendency to standardize space systems and subsystems. The argument for doing so is to spread the non-recurring cost of development over a large base and thereby avoid frequent investments in new designs. But one also pays a price for constraining different missions to use the same system. The alternate is to develop a very expensive system that suits all needs.

This important lesson was learned by the Air Force in its Inertial Upper Stage Program, which was to serve as a universal payload carrier from Shuttle altitude to higher orbits. It began as a simple two stage, solid propellant vehicle that would cost several million dollars. When the requirements of all the missions IUS was to serve were imposed on the design, the recurring cost rose past fifty million dollars. The IUS became the largest common denominator of all user requirements. The point to note is that the cost of adapting to many missions can easily overwhelm the savings of a common design.

In the meantime, a better idea had emerged. It was called Integral Propulsion. The idea was to use the satellite's own guidance system and add a simple rocket to the satellite. The Intelsat VI competition showed that Integral Propulsion was substantially cheaper than a separate stage. The Air Force itself now uses Integral Propulsion for some of its missions rather than the IUS.

The NASA standard module program of ten years ago withered because it tried to freeze technology. It, too, paid an enormous price for generalized solutions.

INTERDEPENDENCY

Space technology and space programs have been instruments of American foreign policy for thirty years. From the beginning, the United States shared space technology with its friends. Our spacecraft carried experiments from other countries. We supported other countries with free rocket launchings. We donated our communication satellite technology to promote the growth of Intelsat.

We established a joint program with the Europeans to build two large spacecraft that would fly to Jupiter and then explore the solar system in three dimensions. The tragedy is that we had to abandon the construction of our spacecraft for budget reasons. Our free shuttle launch of the European vehicle has been delayed almost four years. What began as an exciting joint venture has turned into a difficult situation. International space cooperation is sometimes helpful, sometimes not. The criterion for success is that both sides be able to meet their obligations.

There is a second complication. The strong leadership of NASA is coming into increasing conflict with the rising capabilities and aspirations of other space organizations. This became apparent in Spacelab with the Europeans feeling that they had contributed a great deal in return for too few flights. This came home to rest in the difficult negotiations to generate international participation for the Space Station and SDI.

In the early days of the American space program, a policy decision was made to keep the military and civil space programs entirely separate. The Russians made a different decision and beat us into space with Sputnik. Our original policy of separation was inverted over the next twenty years and DOD was persuaded to fly all its military satellites on the NASA shuttle. That bond is now broken. It is curious how the interdependency between NASA and DOD has gone from one extreme to another -- and back again.

The point of this discussion is that we should retain a certain skepticism about interdependency. There are times when it is the logical thing to do. It can avoid unwarranted duplication. The concern is that symbolic cooperation must not replace sensible joint ventures.

LAUNCH VEHICLES

For sixteen years, the centerpiece of NASA's launch vehicle program was the Space Shuttle. We invested almost forty billion dollars in it. NASA sought and received a monopoly grant from the Carter Administration to launch all future military, scientific, and commercial satellites with the Shuttle. Three years ago, all spacecraft were being designed to fly on the Shuttle. The production lines for Delta and Atlas Centaur rockets were being closed. A last order of ten Titan rockets had been placed in 1985 over the objections of NASA. We were rapidly putting all our eggs in one basket. The stage was set for a disaster and it was not long in coming.

The United States dramatically changed its space launch policy after the Challenger loss. Commercial users of Shuttle were told that their reservation had been cancelled and that they should make other arrangements. The exclusive commitment of DOD to Shuttle was abandoned. The Air Force bought thirteen additional Titan rockets to augment the ten then on order. It chose the Delta II as its new medium launch vehicle and ordered twenty in the first buy. It has ordered eleven Atlas 2 rockets. It is refurbishing fifty Titan II rockets to launch small payloads. Scientific satellites are in storage awaiting future Shuttle assignments or possible switch to Titan.

One never could have imagined such a dramatic change in such a short time. That it was needed is not in doubt. The problem is that space programs have long lead times and cannot adapt to rapid shifts in policy. We are now paying a terrible price for committing all space missions to Shuttle. But we should learn as we pay.

Santayana reminds us that those who do not read history are condemned to repeat it. Looking back in time, we were wildly optimistic about Shuttle's launch rate: six flights per year growing to sixty. NASA was optimistic about demand, too. In 1977, it estimated that almost 600 Shuttle flights would be needed between 1980 and 1991. Eight years later, the estimate was 165. The need forecast for 1988 alone dropped from fifty-eight to twenty. The planned flights for 1988 have fallen from sixty to one.

We are rapidly reestablishing the diversified launch vehicle capability we once abandoned. We have three Shuttles, plus production lines running for Titan, Delta and Atlas Centaur. The Space Shuttles should be husbanded as limited and precious assets. Only they can carry forward our manned program. Only they can provide the unique space services of repair, refurbishment, and retrieval. These missions plus the backlog of spacecraft that can only fly on Shuttles will keep Shuttle busy for many years to come. Conversely, unloading transportation jobs from Shuttle will make its core program more productive and safe.

The next step in expendable launch vehicles is the important decision. The SDI program has defined a need for a new booster that can lift large payloads into space at economical rates to support a proposed deployment. The Air Force has funded studies for an Advanced Launch System that will serve SDI and its own large payload needs. NASA is proposing to develop an unmanned rocket based on Shuttle technology (Shuttle C) to transport supplies and equipment to the proposed Space Station. Much larger boosters would be required for manned missions to the Moon or Mars.

The Aerospace Plane has been suggested for this role, but its

62

technology and performance are too uncertain to commit our space program to it. It seems far more likely that our new heavy lift capability will emerge from traditional rocket technology.

My view is that valid requirements do not support the development of a new large booster today. A manned mission to Mars or a return to the Moon is far from approved. The Space Station is not yet a national commitment. SDI needs a large booster only if it is deployed in space and that is several debates away. Approved DOD and NASA programs need nothing beyond the capability that Shuttle and improved versions of Titan can provide. There is simply no basis now for yet another "infrastructure" investment.

EARTH OBSERVATION

Observing the earth from space has enormous significance for national security, commerce and science. The most important military mission is high resolution surveillance, which was publicly announced by President Carter. Missile warning satellites stationed in geosynchronous orbit provide vital stability in the nuclear age. These missions are generously funded by DOD.

A different kind of surface observation has been conducted by NASA and NOAA under the Landsat program. Landsat resolution is limited by government agreement. However, by observing the earth in different spectral bands and by measuring the absolute energy in each band very accurately, useful agricultural and exploration services have been provided to American and foreign users. France and the Soviet Union now operate similar systems and other countries have announced plans to do so.

The American Landsat service was commercialized several years ago. This is a good time to reconsider that decision. Three choices are available: (1) Continue the present government funded "commercial" service; (2) Renationalize the system and operate it as a public service; or (3) Exploit its inherent similarity to military reconnaissance, add the Landsat cameras to military satellites, and separate the Landsat data from military information on the ground. There are institutional pressures in DOD and State that would resist the third option.

Weather satellites present a different situation, but it too is anomalous. Both NOAA and DOD have operated American low altitude weather satellites for twenty-five years. The spacecraft are virtually the same and come off a common production line. These revisiting spacecraft in low orbit are supplemented by an international civilian network of geosynchronous satellites that provide continuous coverage. Two are maintained by the U.S., one by Japan, one by Europe, and a fifth has been promised but never established by the USSR. The satellite weather service is too valuable, too fragile, and too expensive to continue as we are. For the low altitude coverage, we are overfacilitized. A combination of NOAA and DOD low altitude spacecraft is logical. For the high altitude coverage, we are dependent on foreign partners who do not always share our goals.

We should either establish a unilateral American system or create a genuine international operating system. Intelsat is a good model for how an international system could work. A single entity would raise capital from participating nations and buy spacecraft, launchers, and operating support.

New technology developments are desirable for both weather forecasting and Landsat coverage. The resolution and sensitivity of high altitude satellites should be enhanced to provide long-range forecasting and storm warning capability. Landsat should have its resolution upgraded. A commercial incentive to sponsor these developments is missing. They should be funded by the government or by an international consortium, as Intelsat and Inmarsat now fund their own developments.

A third class of earth observing space systems study the Earth's atmosphere and environment. The ozone hole above Antarctica and the progressive drought in America have focused increasing public attention on the crucial role played by the upper atmosphere. Satellite systems are the best way to study these phenomena. The U.S. Upper Atmosphere Research Satellite is to be launched in 1991 and other spacecraft are being planned here and abroad. The Global Geospace Science program will place spacecraft in high earth orbit to monitor the plasma sheath around the Earth and its relation to the sun. But this building and planning have been long drawn out. The Earth's upper atmosphere is an urgent worldwide problem. Its study and solution should be a worldwide effort.

The area of earth observation is a difficult one in which to make clean, clear policy recommendations. This is because it is closely coupled to what the DOD does and what other nations do. Nevertheless, it is an area that cries out for examination. My feeling is that we should either: (1) Provide a failsafe,

64

unilateral American capability, or (2) Create a truly international system based on the Intelsat model. We now have the worst features of both approaches by being halfway in between.

PLANETARY EXPLORATION

The United States has led the world in exploring the solar system. We have sent flyby encounter missions to all the planets except Pluto. We sent instrumented landers to Mars and the Moon, and probes to Venus. We have sent a probe out of the solar system. We are building a large spacecraft that will go into orbit about Jupiter and send a probe into its atmosphere. We are building spacecraft that will go into orbit around Mars and Venus.

Other nations are getting into the act. The Soviets have explored Venus extensively with landers. They are now going to Mars and its moons. The Japanese, Russians, and Europeans each sent probes to intercept Comet Halley.

There is important work that remains to be done. Eventually we shall want to send probes into the atmospheres of Saturn, Uranus, and Neptune. Moons of the outer planets are solid and landable, in contrast to the large gaseous planets they circle. They provide stable observation platforms and are of interest in themselves. Mercury and the region near the sun has been explored only once. Sample return from Mars is the next important mission in our region of the solar system.

The American program for planetary exploration has slowed markedly in the last decade. This was caused by the fiscal demands of other programs, management preoccupation with Shuttle, and the lack of clear purpose. We have been living off the long life of earlier spacecraft. Our current program is characterized by a series of non-redundant, single missions. Many of them suffer from the "bigger is better" syndrome. All are plagued by the Shuttle standdown.

A sensible approach is to decide how much we the people are prepared to invest each year in exploring the solar system. With a stable budget, scientists can lay out a plan for the systematic exploration of the planets. Such a plan has been put forward by the Space Science Board. Such a program should be pursued with the clear understanding that its overruns would simply delay the program, not tax others. With fixed launch windows, this would inflict a strong discipline on those who specify, manage, and build such systems. Conversely, the planetary program should be assured that problems elsewhere in the civil program would not be solved at its expense.

These missions should move to expendable launch vehicles from the Shuttle. Astronauts play no vital role in launching planetary missions. In fact, they impose harsh safety requirements on the high energy upper stages that are usually required. This was the reason that the Shuttle Centaur stage was cancelled soon after the Challenger loss. With an expendable launch policy, future groundings of the Shuttle would not interrupt the essential rhythm of spacecraft building and launching to the planets.

ASTRONOMY

The NASA program for astronomy is an exciting one. It is dominated by the two Great Observatories: the Hubble Space Telescope and the Gamma Ray Observatory. Both are programmed to fly on the Shuttle and are now on hold. In addition to the frustration of delay, there is another problem.

When the Hubble Space Telescope was conceived in the early 1970s, it was thought that it could provide a unique capability in the optical and ultraviolet bands of the spectrum, and be able to see deep into the universe because it will observe from above earth's obscuring atmosphere. With its 2.4 meter mirror, it will produce an angular resolution of 50 milliarcseconds. The terrestrial Keck Telescope being built in Hawaii is being designed to produce this accuracy using active mirror control of its 10 meter reflector, but only in the optical regime. HST will remain unsurpassed in the ultraviolet. As technology advances, terrestrial telescopes can increasingly compete with some of the Great Observatories, and they are substantially cheaper. Hubble cost one and one half billion dollars, while Keck is budgeted for 85 million. Even with both great telescopes, the demand of astronomers for observing time will still exceed the availability by factors of two or three. It is important to launch the Great Observatories as soon as we safely can.

We need to find out quickly what are the real advantages of operating in space. If there is a commanding advantage, we should plan a second generation of observatories. The next level of performance is that required to see the planets of other solar systems. This will require a resolution of 5 milliarcseconds or ten times that of Hubble.

There are some kinds of astronomy that can only be done from space, because the Earth's atmosphere absorbs the signals one

66

wants to detect. Very high energy radiation from stars are one example and a NASA program to develop an X-ray observatory has just begun. Low energy infrared radiation is another important way to study the universe and is best done from space vehicles.

There is another branch of astronomy for which space provides a unique advantage: radio astronomy. Radio astronomers have been probing deeper into the universe with terrestrial antennas for forty years. With very long baseline interferometry, they have located and imaged cosmic radio sources. They now use the full diameter of the earth for this stellar direction finding.

To take the next step, one must go into space. If we build a radio astronomy antenna on a satellite and fly it away from the earth, we could provide a baseline almost equal to the diameter of the earth's orbit around the sun. Much of the technology for such systems exists. NASA knows how to build spacecraft that fly around the solar system and knows how to communicate with them. DOD knows how to unfurl large antennas and build sensitive receivers. Combining these capabilities, we could take the next important step in radio astronomy.

Like planetary exploration, the astronomy program should have a sheltered budget. Its absolute level should be worked out between OMB, Congress, and the science community. Once established, it should remain a confident benchmark against which long range planning can be maintained.

MANNED PROGRAMS

Manned space flight has been the centerpiece of the NASA program from its beginning. It has also been the playing field on which we have contested the Russians for world leadership. They were the first to put men and women in space. We went first to the moon and are still unmatched in that remarkable feat. They have pursued a continuing program of small earth orbiting Space Stations and have learned a great deal about man's ability to work in space for long periods.

We chose the shuttle as our step beyond the moon. It provides a routine way to reach low earth orbit and return. It can stay only a short time in orbit, but has done a variety of useful experiments. In addition, the shuttle crews have performed remarkable, unplanned repairs on stranded satellites.

It is important to note that manned space operations have played no role in the military space program since the Manned

Orbiting Laboratory (MOL) Program was cancelled two decades ago. It is the DOD view that men are neither needed nor desired for their missions. The commercial world shares this view. So does the scientific community.

NASA now wishes to build a large Space Station in low earth orbit. This will provide a long duration manned facility for scientific observations and material processing experiments. The Space Station received initial Presidential approval, but is now bogged down in Congress where initial enthusiasm has been softening. This is reflected in media concern and in public apathy. The program is handicapped by a lack of clear purpose. This is aggravated by cost growth and schedule delay, as initial optimism has given way to stern reality.

One problem with Space Station is that we are not sure why we are building it. The Space Station now planned by NASA will be an enormous project. It will absorb most of NASA's talent and money for the next decade. It will effectively block other manned efforts.

The Space Station will travel in low earth orbit, not far from the equator. There are few space jobs that are done in this orbit. Communication and warning missions are done in high earth orbit. Navigation satellites fly almost as high. All earth observation missions fly in polar orbits.

The Space Station can do jobs that are orbit-independent. The processing of materials in a zero gravity environment is one such mission. Astronomical observations is another. Data on astronaut physiology over a long period can be acquired in a Space Station. The Space Station can also play an important role as a "Base Camp" for manned missions beyond the earth. However, the present Station does not include a Base Camp capability because it is so difficult to anticipate the requirements of unplanned future missions.

While we are thinking about manned space flight, we should consider two other missions: (1) Returning to the Moon, and (2) Manned visits to Mars. Both are technically feasible. Both will be very expensive. However, the Moon and Mars are the only places in the solar system where men can land safely. We should decide if we want to send Americans to Mars. If we do, we must decide whether we want to go alone or in a cooperative venture. Whether we collaborate or compete, we need to be ready to start soon. If we invest heavily in Space Station now, we will have effectively made the decision not to go.

I believe that it would be unwise to proceed with the Space

Station at this time. It has not been subjected to the kind of national debate that is appropriate for such a large and exclusive effort. It is without clear purpose. It violates the most important lessons we have learned in the past thirty years. Quite literally, it puts all our eggs in one basket. It is important to involve the American people in this decision. The manned space program is basically their program.

CONCLUSION

If there is a central theme in this chapter, it is that redundancy and resiliency are unambiguous virtues. We have recently reestablished those virtues in our launch vehicle program in response to a national tragedy.

We have abandoned these virtues for scientific satellite missions in response to the budget pressures. Today, virtually all of our missions are single string. Some missions require very large spacecraft and the space telescope is an example. But other missions do not. We must avoid bundling missions together, as we did in combining the Galileo Probe and Orbiter missions. We should insist on the budgetary resources and program discipline that will allow us to build two spacecraft for each important mission, as we did in Viking and Voyager.

There is another aspect to redundancy and resiliency. It is institutional. Early in our nuclear program, all weapon designs were conceived, advocated and executed by the Los Alamos National Laboratory. It set the pace and direction of our early program. During the Eisenhower Administration, the DOD became impatient with that direction and pace. The Lawrence Livermore Laboratory was established as a competitive weapons design group. From that day forward, the development of nuclear weapons was vigorous and effective. Ten years later a similar duality was created for certain military space projects for precisely the same reason.

A similar situation may exist today. NASA enjoys a virtual monopoly on both manned and unmanned civil space activities. It falls to NASA to originate, advocate and execute our civil space program. Our current disappointment with this program may be the result of a monopoly gone astray. However, I do not believe that it makes sense to duplicate NASA to achieve competitive thinking.

I do believe that the civil space program suffers from one major deficiency. It receives too little policy guidance from the Executive Branch and Congress. Absent clear policy guidance,

NASA tries to generate programs and sell them in an increasingly difficult environment. If I am correct in this assessment, I hope that this chapter will identify the issues and encourage others to think hard about a difficult question.

ACKNOWLEDGMENTS

The author wishes to thank Cicely Wheelon, R. Herres, L. Allen, W. Perry, B. Murray, J. McElroy, B. Miller, L.A. Hyland, D.J. Kutyna and R.F. Mettler, for valuable comments on a draft. However, the viewpoints in this chapter are strictly those of the author.

PART TWO

Programs and Problems

The four essays which follow focus on major elements of the civilian space program: space transportation systems, the space science program, the space application programs, and the institution needed to have a program, i.e. the infrastructure. Together these elements account for most of the civilian space budget and resources. Space applications also involve many other government and private sector organizations.

These chapters present independent critiques of current program and policy issues by individuals with extensive involvement in the civilian space program.

Richard DalBello of the Office of Technology Assessment believes that decisions on whether and when to proceed on major new transportation initiatives should be taken in the context of what the Nation wants to achieve in space. Although new launch systems could be developed that would reduce future launch operating costs, "reducing life-cycle cost is not easy and reducing program costs is harder still." A major conclusion of his study is that "it is not prudent or necessary to develop new technologies simply because we can, nor is it prudent to support our large space institutions simply because they already exist. The leaders of the United States must decide what they want to do in space and then organize to accomplish these goals."

Riccardo Giacconi, currently the Director of the Hubble Space Telescope Science Institute, is an eminent space scientist with important discoveries in X-ray astronomy. Giacconi's essay is a passionate critique of NASA's current science policies and management practices. He argues that the productivity and effectiveness of NASA's space science programs could be greatly enhanced by loosening coupling between space science and the Shuttle and Station programs.

Marcia S. Smith of the Congressional Research Service addresses the thorny policy and program issues related to development and commercialization of space technology for practical applications. Smith's essay recounts the convoluted history of the attempts to "privatize" the Landsat remote-sensing satellites and the continuing policy dispute over the appropriate government role in the development of advanced communications satellite technology. She points out that policy decisions today are much more complex than in the first decades of the space program: "When space was new and emotions ran high about the potential of space technology for improving everyday life, the question of who was going to develop the technology had an easy answer: NASA. Those days are long since gone."

Science writer M. Mitchell Waldrop discusses the general topics of space infrastructure and space operations, which in his view are likely to "...dominate NASA's budget for as long as any of us can foresee." Waldrop is concerned that the "cost of building and maintaining the hardware makes it harder and harder to do anything with it, like science or applications." Waldrop's chapter addresses what he considers to be the hardware, software and "firmware" of the space program. Commitment to a major piece of infrastructure sets in motion a process that may have quite unexpected consequences. For example, the development of the Space Shuttle has had a major influence in shaping how the public perceives the basic purpose, and hence the future, of what the nation will choose to do in space.

Aside from their critical approaches to the established priorities and methods for carrying out our civilian space program, what do these chapters have in common? All of the authors are convinced that we could do much better in managing our current activities in space research and exploration and clearly believe that the program deserves the efforts required to make it better.

Chapter 4

SPACE TRANSPORTATION AND THE FUTURE OF THE U.S. SPACE PROGRAM

Richard DalBello

IN THE LONG RUN MEN HIT ONLY WHAT THEY AIM AT.

THOREAU

SPACE TRANSPORTATION TECHNOLOGY AND SPACE POLICY

The Office of Technology Assessment[1] (OTA) recently published two reports on space transportation technology. The first report, *Launch Options for the Future: A Buyer's Guide*,[2] analyzed and provided cost estimates for the new launch vehicles that the United States could build. The second report, *Reducing Launch Operations Costs: New Technologies and Practices*,[3] examined how new technologies and management strategies could reduce the cost of vehicle preparation and launch. Although the subject matter of these reports is different, taken together, they make three general points. First:

The United States has the technical ability to develop a range of new, more capable launch vehicles and ground systems, but choosing wisely among these alternatives requires that it first make some hard choices about how it would use these new systems.

Although the United States has many technical opportunities, it is not prepared to pursue them all simultaneously. Choosing wrongly, choosing prematurely, or failing to choose the appropriate

74

space transportation system could waste tens of billions of dollars. For example, a launch system designed to meet current needs would be woefully inadequate to send humans to Mars or to deploy SDI. Conversely, building a launch fleet to support SDI deployment or human exploration of Mars would be an unnecessary extravagance should those programs fail to materialize. In other words, space transportation is generally not an end in itself, but rather, a means to an end.[4] The space transportation systems we build should be appropriate for, and should serve the goals of, our space programs. Yet, there is no clear set of space goals that is widely endorsed by the political leaders and the people of the United States. So, technical solutions are offered to solve problems in programs that have not been endorsed. And while the ensuing debate may be technically sophisticated it is politically irrelevant.

OTA's report on *Launch Options for the Future* examined a range of policy goals and technical solutions and reached several conclusions regarding the relations between goals and transportation needs:

1. If the Nation wishes to limit the future growth of NASA and DoD space programs: then it should maintain existing launch systems and limit expenditures on future development options. This is because current capabilities are adequate to supply both NASA and DoD if the present level of U.S. space activities is maintained or reduced.

2. If the Nation wishes to deploy the Space Station by the mid-90s while maintaining an aggressive NASA science program: then it should continue funding improvements to the Space Shuttle *and/or* begin developing an unpiloted Shuttle vehicle (Shuttle-C). The current Space Shuttle can launch the Space Station, but will do so more effectively with improvements or the assistance of a Shuttle-C. Although Shuttle-C may not be as economical as other new cargo vehicles at high launch rates, it is competitive if only a few heavy-lift missions are required each year.

3. If the Nation wishes to send humans to Mars or establish a base on the moon: then it should commit to the development of a new unpiloted cargo vehicle (Shuttle-C or a cargo vehicle not based on Shuttle technology) and continue research and funding for Shuttle II and the National Aerospace Plane. A commitment to piloted spaceflight will require a Shuttle replacement shortly after the turn of the century. Large planetary missions will also need a new, more economical, cargo vehicle.

4. If the Nation wishes to continue trend of launching heavier

communications, navigation, and reconnaissance satellites and/or pursue an aggressive SDI test program to prepare for eventual deployment: then it should commit to the development of a new unpiloted cargo vehicle not based on Shuttle technology. In theory, current launch systems could be expanded to meet future needs; however, new systems are likely to be more reliable and more cost-effective.

5. If the nation wishes to deploy SDI and/or dramatically increase the number and kind of other military space activities: then it should commit to the development of a new unpiloted cargo vehicle not based on Shuttle technology. This is because current launch systems are neither sufficiently economical to support SDI deployment nor reliable enough to support a dramatically increased military space program.

The second general point made in the OTA reports:

The United States could develop launch systems that would substantially reduce launch operations costs, but reducing life-cycle cost is not as easy and reducing program costs is harder still.

Many informed observers have complained that the U.S. space program costs too much and that reducing the cost of space transportation should be a central concern of our space efforts. OTA's analysis indicates that the United States could develop launch systems that are cheaper to produce and operate than existing systems. However, at low launch rates, where it is difficult to amortize the substantial development cost of these systems, there is no compelling *economic* reason to push for their development.[5] At very high launch rates, where the development cost can be spread over many launches, it makes sense to look to new technologies that can dramatically reduce operations cost. However, launching frequently means the United States would have to be prepared to buy more launches and more payloads for those launches. As a result, space program costs would still be very high, since the money "saved" by flying new vehicles very frequently could be "lost" by dramatically increased spending for payloads and additional flights.

Current methods for estimating launch system costs are subjective and unreliable. Improving the science of cost estimation should be part of any launch vehicle or technology development program. Even if future launch vehicle demand were known, estimated costs of launch systems would still be highly uncertain because the United States' space transportation operations experience is limited compared to other mature industries -- such as commercial aviation -- and a highly detailed data base is unavailable. Although recent NASA and Air Force studies have improved cost estimating models, much work is still needed to find and aggregate historical cost data, record and analyze more system details, make uncertainties more explicit, and develop the means to estimate the effects of new technologies on manufacturing costs and launch systems operations.

Finally, large development projects for new space transportation systems are not likely to achieve their cost or technical objectives without continuity in commitment and funding. The ultimate cost of any large system depends on how it is purchased. The nature of the annual budgeting and appropriations process often causes yearly fluctuations in the continuity of development funds, or delays in purchasing systems and facilities. These effects can produce significant increases in the cost of large systems.

Spending scarce resources wisely should always be a motivating concern. However, focusing narrowly on reducing the cost of space transportation may not be a productive strategy. It is more important that the U.S. define policy goals that can be broadly supported by the Government and the American people. At present, the costs of indecision in the U.S. space program may exceed the costs of inefficient operations in one or another program.

The third general point made in the OTA reports:

It will be difficult to improve the way the United States manages its launch systems without making significant changes to the institutions currently responsible for those systems.

Current U.S. space management practices result from a launch operations philosophy that emphasizes long-lived, expensive payloads, high-performance launchers, very high reliability, and low launch rates. The United States is now in the difficult position of attempting to retain its high-technology, high-performance approach to payloads and vehicles while attaining Soviet-style routine, lower cost access to space. Many experts argue that to really change the way the U.S. manages its launch systems would require substantial alterations to the launch "culture" that has developed over the years in both NASA and the Air Force. Two principal paths have been suggested for accomplishing this cultural change. First, some argue that the

United States ought to set up an independent government launch agency whose skills and creativity would be focused on the task of making launch operations more efficient and less costly. Others argue that it makes more sense to turn launch operations for all new launch systems over to the private sector and to purchase launch services, rather than vehicles, from the private sector for existing ELVs. Critical to both of these suggestions is the assumption that dramatic change cannot take place within the existing, tradition-bound space agencies.

The financial success of the European Space Agency's Ariane launch vehicle is evidence of the wisdom of separating the launch vehicle developers from the launch vehicle operators. When planning for the development and operation of the Ariane, the European partners decided early to separate the function of launcher development and operations. ESA, using the French space agency (CNES) as a technical manager, devoted its attention to building a capable and efficient launch vehicle. Arianespace, S.A., a private French corporation focused on marketing and developing cost-effective launch operations procedures. Because Arianespace had to compete from its inception in the international marketplace, it had strong commercial incentives to minimize total launch vehicle costs. ESA and CNES, on the other hand, had to compete technically with the launch vehicles of the United States and the Soviet Union, and therefore had a strong incentive to build the most capable launch vehicle that it could. By creating a division between the authority for development and operations, both institutions were given a power base from which to argue their own technical and financial case. Neither institution could have proceeded without the help and expertise of the other, and each contributed to the development of a launch system that is both capable and cost effective.

The primary reason for institutionalizing the tension between launcher development and operations is the belief that it will enhance innovation and lower costs. In the United States, such a division of responsibility might have several advantages. First, launch costs would be more visible and comprehensible than they are now. Second, since the launch agency or company would focus on launching vehicles for its clients, rather than on vehicle or payload development, it would have a stake in limiting the number and extent of vehicle modifications -- a major cost driver in today's systems. Finally, because the launch operations agency or company would be competing for launch services in the international market, it would have considerable incentive to be innovative in cost reduction practices.

INSTITUTIONAL ALTERNATIVES

The bottom line of much of the above analysis is quite simple -- ends should define means and *not vice-versa*. The U.S. space program is not the technology it employs, nor is it the institutions that employ that technology. The U.S. space program is what the United States wants to do in space. Technology and institutions should be means to that end. Sadly, a national consensus on the "ends" of the U.S. space program does not exist.

One often hears the proposed NASA Space Station referred to as the "next logical step." The statement begs the question, "next logical step to what?" The answer to this question has been clear, at least to NASA, for decades. In the late 1960s, NASA developed plans to build a reusable launch vehicle, to build a Space Station, and to send humans to explore the moon and the planets. Given the success of Apollo, these plans seemed a reasonable and logical continuation of the bold course originally charted by the Kennedy and Johnson Administrations. However, global conflicts, tightening budgets, the technical complexity of the Space Shuttle project, a loss of U.S. competitiveness in key industries, and a growing public skepticism about the near-term value of space exploration have altered the Nation's perception of NASA's long-range plans.

Nonetheless, NASA's vision of its long-range goals has remained relatively constant throughout the years. The technologies and the programs NASA has supported -- the Space Shuttle and the proposed Space Station -- reflect the agency's commitment to its original objectives. The luke-warm support the Reagan Administration gave to the Space Station, growing Congressional skepticism about the cost of both the Shuttle and the proposed Station, and the modest support that the Station has received from the scientists and the public, all point to a need to seriously reexamine what it is that we are committed to in space. The Reagan Administration in its final declaration of U.S. space policy identified "expanding human presence and activity beyond Earth orbit" as a "long-range goal." However, the only practical manifestation of this commitment was a modestly funded technology development program. This somewhat tentative handling of what is arguably the cornerstone of the NASA vision of the future is strong evidence of the mismatch between the space goals that NASA would generate and the goals that this nation seems prepared to endorse.

What then are the central goals of the U.S. space program and what is the role that human exploration should play? More importantly, how should the answer to these questions affect NASA's size, structure, and budget? Providing adequate answers to these questions is well beyond the scope of this paper, however it is possible to sketch the broad outlines of two possible alternatives:

A Bold Commitment to Human Exploration

The United States could decide that it wants to maintain a strong commitment to human exploration of the Solar System and beyond. From an institutional perspective, the large, geographically diverse, multi-talented NASA that currently exists would be well-suited to this task. The technology to accomplish this goal does not now exist but, if sufficient resources are made available, it could. The missing ingredient to this formula is, of course, a national willingness to increase NASA's budget dramatically. Sending humans to space is, and will continue to be, a phenomenally expensive undertaking. Still, it is not so expensive that the United States could not afford it, and such a program would have some strong advantages. First, a truly bold space program would be a source of tremendous national pride, it would be consonant with our pioneering spirit, and it might recapture the sense of national technical dynamism that was so apparent during the heady days of Apollo. Sending humans to space, like the building of the Gothic cathedrals, is an activity that is hard to rationalize economically but which speaks to something deeper and more profound in the human spirit. Second, whether the United States acted alone or with other countries, a bold space program would allow the United States to reassert its role as a leader in space technology and exploration. It can be argued that leadership in space contributes to leadership in technology and world politics. Finally, the human exploration of the planets would contribute broadly to our knowledge of the universe and make possible life enhancing advances in science.

A Commitment to Science and Unmanned Exploration

NASA could be an organization that was committed to research, robotic exploration and science and which specifically rejected the goal of extensive human space exploration. Dramatically reducing the man-in-space component of NASA's activities could have a tremendous effect on NASA the institution. Shuttle activities and their related expenses could be curtailed, much of the work of the NASA centers which focuses on human spaceflight could be eliminated, and the proposed Space Station could be canceled or dramatically altered. Overall, a NASA science agency would be smaller, perhaps by half, than the current NASA and could operate on an equally reduced budget. Other than responding to the current fashion of budget reductions, a simpler space science agency might actually be able to do more interesting scientific work. Much of the current NASA budget is dedicated to operating the Space Shuttle and a greater share of future NASA budgets will go to operating the Space Station. These large operations expenses would be reduced or eliminated, freeing up the resources and energy necessary to mount a space science program that is second to none. Such a restructured NASA would still be able to explore the solar system, but it would do so using robots instead of astronauts. In addition to leading in space exploration, a greatly enhanced program of robotic exploration could regain for the United States its dominant position in the key commercial industries of automation, and robotics. Of course, not all the changes that would occur would be positive. People would lose jobs, NASA centers might be closed, important skills and new transportation technologies might be lost, and the U.S. would forego the challenge of sending humans to the planets. Whether the benefits of a smaller, science-oriented NASA would outweigh the losses would be a subject requiring close scientific and political scrutiny.

CONCLUSION

Is there anything really wrong with the U.S. space program? Why can't we just continue the way we have been going? The answer is that the current system requires NASA to pretend that its space goals are the nation's space goals. As a result, promises are made that cannot be kept and large expensive programs are started that have little chance of full and adequate funding.

This paper argues that it is not prudent or necessary to develop new technologies simply because we can, nor is it prudent to support our large space institutions simply because they already exist. The leaders of the United States must decide what they want to do in space and then organize to accomplish these goals. This paper also argues that the United States is either committed to the human exploration of space or it isn't; if it is, then it should give NASA the resources it needs to carry out this objective, if it isn't, then it should redefine its goals and restructure NASA.

Some may argue that this choice is too stark, that it is a caricature of reality. They will argue that the real issue is finding the appropriate balance between the human exploration of space and other scientific, national security, and commercial activities.

This paper rejects those arguments. NASA is not the size it is, does not require the personnel and budgets that it does because it wants to pursue space science, commerce, or advanced R&D. The manned space program is not simply part of what NASA does, it is the essence of what NASA is. Total annual Space Shuttle expenses amount to roughly half of the current $10 billion NASA budget. Building the NASA Space Station will involve additional annual expenditures at least as great. The price is too high to defer a serious national debate on this subject.

This paper argues that the only convincing rationale for the Space Shuttle and for the proposed Space Station is to learn to live and work in space and the only convincing reason to learn to live and work in space is to gain the skills necessary to send humans to the planets. One can argue that manned spaceflight contributes to national security, but DoD has struggled mightily to free itself from the Shuttle and Space Station programs. One can argue that the Shuttle and the Space Station will lead to commercial opportunities, yet in seven years of Shuttle operations not one serious commercial company has developed and none are in the wings. One can argue that the Shuttle and the Station will lead to great scientific advances, but the science community had to be dragged kicking and screaming into both programs and there is evidence to suggest that most space science can be carried out more efficiently on expendable launch vehicles.

This paper is emphatically *not* arguing that the Shuttle and the Space Station are bad ideas. It is arguing they are excellent ideas for a nation that intends to have its citizens explore the solar system. However, if the United States is not prepared to support actively that goal then it had better think hard about why it wants a civilian space program.

NOTES

1. The Office of Technology Assessment was established by

Congress to provide congressional committees with analyses of technical issues.

2. U.S. Congress, Office of Technology Assessment, *Launch Options for the Future: A Buyer's Guide*, OTA-ISC-383 (Washington, D.C.: U.S. Government Printing Office, July 1988).

3. U.S. Congress, Office of Technology Assessment, *Reducing Launch Operations Costs: New Technologies and Practices*, OTA-TM-ISC-28 (Washington, D.C.: U.S. Government Printing Office, September 1988).

4. Some degree of non-program specific, advanced technology work is essential if we are to prepare adequately for the future. Whether or not this technology work needs to be incorporated in an operational launch vehicle is another question. Some argue that the Space Shuttle was so dramatic a step in the evolution of space transportation systems that it should be regarded as an end in itself. Similar arguments are now being made regarding the National Aerospace Plane.

5. Non-economic criteria such as a desire for increased capability or reliability might provide the necessary motivation for a new launch vehicle development even if costs were to remain the same.

Chapter 5

SCIENCE AND TECHNOLOGY POLICY: SPACE SCIENCE STRATEGIES FOR THE 1990s

Riccardo Giacconi

NEW IDEAS ARE NOT ONLY THE ENEMIES OF OLD ONES; THEY ALSO APPEAR OFTEN IN AN EXTREMELY UNACCEPTABLE FORM.

C.G. JUNG

I MUST CREATE A SYSTEM, OR BE ENSLAV'D BY ANOTHER MAN'S.

W. BLAKE

INTRODUCTION

One need only read the major newspapers and periodicals after the Challenger accident to know that something is seriously wrong with the space program. There were no major launches between early 1986 and the fall of 1988. For all practical purposes, the U.S. had no access to space during that time and has limited access now, while the USSR, the European Space Agency (ESA) and Japan are forging ahead. The very serious mistake of NASA in relying solely on the Shuttle as the sole space transportation system for military, commercial and scientific payloads is broadly appreciated and the remedy of turning to a "mixed fleet" (in NASA's parlance) of Shuttle plus unmanned expendable launch vehicles (ELVs) appears immediately obvious. Further policy discussions center on budgetary issues, on the ratio between expenditures for manned versus unmanned programs, and on the desirability, from this point of view, of making a start toward the Space Station.

One often hears, particularly from NASA sources, that the problems of the space program are due to the lack of commitment from the U.S. as a whole. That is, NASA is asked to do the impossible with inadequate resources. It is asserted that the supremacy of the U.S. in space can be re-established only by doubling or tripling NASA's budget.

My point of view, which is shared by many other scientists, is that one has to look deeper than this to understand our current problems. Without appropriate reforms, no amount of money that is likely to be approved by Congress can lead us to a successful program. Conversely, it is not clear that the amount we have currently available, for instance in the space sciences, can be properly administered under present policy.

In the body of the text I will attempt a first-cut diagnostic of the ills of the U.S. space program with particular emphasis on our concerns in the space sciences. As a conclusion I will offer a few recommendations which if adopted would go a long way toward making the necessary changes. There are primarily three areas where change is needed:

-- First, human exploration of space: We need a clearly defined set of goals for the human exploration of space. Also, a recognition that the scientific community should be more deeply involved in selection of future steps and more supportive in defining the scientific strategies to acquire the necessary knowledge. Finally, we need a recognition that many national needs can not and should not be addressed in the context of manned exploration.

-- Second, space science: We need a strong and independent space science program which is accepted as having a justification and a rationale of its own and not only as a subservient component of manned exploration. Such a program would be based mainly on the use of ELV's and, by accepting greater risks, could substantially reduce single mission costs. This would allow the U.S. science community to return to a position of leadership in the world.

-- Third, organization: The management and structure of NASA as well as the relationship between the three partners in the space science enterprise (government, industry and university) must be carefully re-evaluated and where necessary changed to improve the efficiency with which the entire program is carried out.

STATUS

Four illustrations taken from the November, 1986 report by the Space and Earth Science Advisory Committee of the NASA Advisory Council can be used as a starting point.[1] Figure 1 of the report shows funding in 1982 dollars for NASA and the Office of Space Science and Applications (OSSA), the ratio between OSSA and total NASA, and the use of the money in OSSA. Figure 2 from the report shows the decrease in launches since 1967. Figure 3 is the history of the time interval between the Announcement of Opportunity (AO) and mission launch for major OSSA missions. Finally, Figure 4 is a summation of discipline aspirations versus available funding.

What is the picture that emerges?

-- Figure 1 shows that the OSSA budget has fluctuated a lot but always in a healthy range of about 1 to 1.5 billion a year. (This is several times the ESA science budget, and more than ten times the Japanese science budget.)
-- Figure 2 shows that notwithstanding the above, fewer and fewer launch opportunities have been available for space scientists. This presents particular problems for training the new generations of scientists and engineers. (The next few years may see a burst of science missions launched, but this will represent the backlog accumulated during the Shuttle standdown, not a fundamental change.)
-- Figure 3 shows that the interval between scientific start of a mission and its launch steadily grew from a few years to more than ten years; this also is a problem for training.
-- And finally, Figure 4 shows that the cost of the desired program much exceeds available resources.

Many of the problems above are the direct result of a tight dependence on Shuttle decreed by NASA. The decision effectively to abolish the rocket and small satellite scientific programs and to conduct all small science (which is defined as small cost, fast response) with Shuttle sortie missions produced the following effects:

-- Even small payloads became quite expensive because of safety considerations and integration costs. These costs doubled the total costs of experiments on Shuttle as compared to previous launchers.

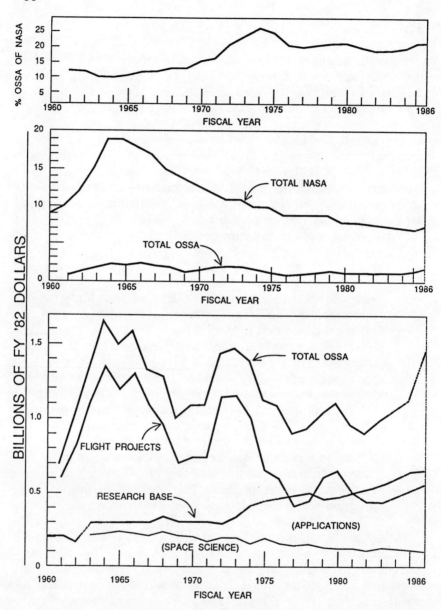

Figure 1.   *Funding History of NASA and the Office of Space Science and Applications (OSSA).*

SOURCE: *The Crisis in Space and Earth Science: A Time for a New Commitment.*
A Report by the Space and Earth Science Advisory Committee, NASA Advisory
Council. November 1986.

LAUNCH RATE

SUCCESSFUL SPACE & EARTH SCIENCE LAUNCHES BY YEAR

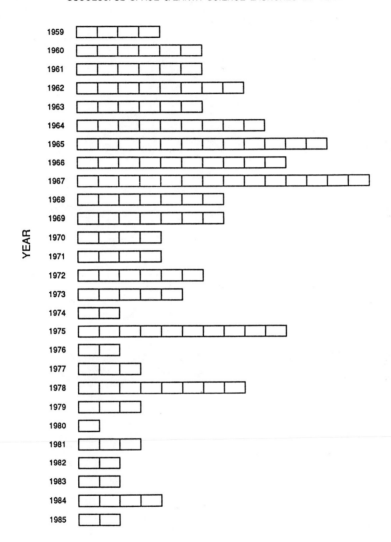

Figure 2.   Launch Rate.

SOURCE: The Crisis in Space and Earth Science: A Time for a New Commitment.
A Report by the Space and Earth Science Advisory Committee, NASA Advisory
Council. November 1986.

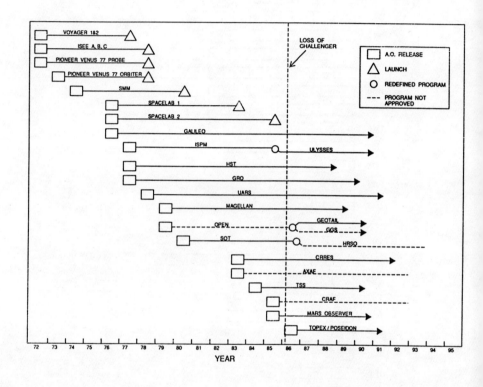

Figure 3. *History of the Time Interval Between Release of an Announcement of Opportunity (AO) and Launch of Major OSSA Missions.*

SOURCE: The Crisis in Space and Earth Science: A Time for a New Commitment. A Report by the Space and Earth Science Advisory Committee, NASA Advisory Council. November 1986.

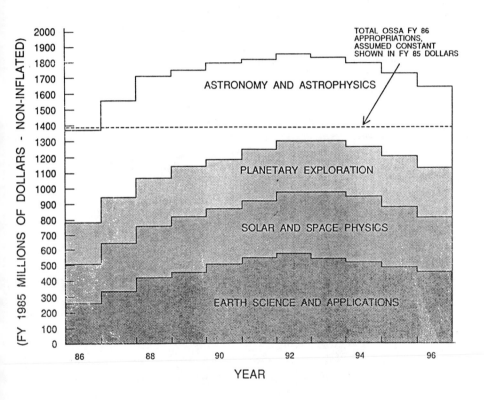

Figure 4. The Summation of Discipline Aspirations.

SOURCE: *The Crisis in Space and Earth Science: A Time for a New Commitment.* A Report by the Space and Earth Science Advisory Committee, NASA Advisory Council. November 1986.

-- A very large amount (perhaps a million pounds) of scientific payload got built, but never flew and never will.[2]

The decision by NASA to use Space Shuttle as the booster for all free flying payloads created additional problems here exemplified in two cases:

-- The Galileo project became the victim of the inappropriate decision to launch it with Shuttle. The Centaur upper stage for Shuttle was cancelled due to severe safety concerns. The current mission plan involving use of a low energy upper stage and the delays in the Shuttle program caused by the Challenger accident, now will force a further several-year delay in reaching the objective, i.e. Jupiter.
-- The Hubble Space Telescope (HST) will be the first of the Great Observatories[*] to be launched in the 1989 to 1999 period to permit astronomical observations over the entire spectrum of wavelengths. At program initiation and given the extremely optimistic view then prevalent at NASA about Shuttle launch rates (perhaps sixty per year) and costs, it appeared sensible to plan for permanent observatories to be carried aloft by Shuttle and maintained for long periods of time (twenty years) by Shuttle astronauts. HST was, in fact, designed to depend for survival on frequent servicing. It is obvious now that the servicing costs (accumulated over time) will exceed the cost of a whole new observatory every ten years and that the availability of the Shuttle may be questionable. Furthermore, the cost of development of HST has exceeded by several times the original estimates and its deployment has been delayed about six years from the date originally anticipated.

DIAGNOSTIC I

To extract from these episodes a common thread is not terribly

---

[*] The four great observatories will observe in four different regimes as follows: in the gamma ray regime with Gamma Ray Observatory (GRO), x-ray with Advanced X-ray Astronomical Facility (AXAF), optical and ultraviolet with Hubble Space Telescope (HST), and infrared with Shuttle Infrared Telescope Facility (SIRTF).

difficult. NASA's days of glory were in the 1960s when the Kennedy commitment to place a man on the moon by 1970 was being executed. In the flush of success at having beaten the Russians, very few critics questioned the program's validity. Important questions were never asked: what would Apollo lead to beyond the spectacular achievement? What would be the next goal in space? Could this be the first step to an evolutionary program leading somewhere? To all of the above there were no easy answers. After Apollo we were left with a large bureaucracy (NASA) which, since then, has been concerned mainly with survival. It is unfortunate that NASA's administrators conceived of NASA survival mainly as the maintenance of the manned program. When, at the end of the 60s, no new major national space goal had been set by the Administration and therefore funding could no longer be maintained at the levels prevailing during the Apollo era, the Shuttle program appeared as a step toward a long range manned program which would sustain institutional and industrial interest in the NASA program. (This approach is in marked contrast to the Soviet use of proven technology in carrying out its program. Their success proves that a valid space program does not require continuous innovation in the transportation system.)

Reality and technical truth were the victims of the selling campaign for Shuttle. Costs of $30 Million per Shuttle launch and up to sixty launches per year were talked about as if they had been carefully assessed and achievable goals.

For a brief period, under the Carter Administration, there was an opportunity for reassessing the Shuttle program which was encountering technical difficulties, delays and overruns. However, the end seemed to be in sight and the decision was made to continue the program without substantive change. An additional $900 Million dollars would soon be required to solve problems which had not been fully appreciated, leading to a certain lack of credibility in Congress. NASA, however, persevered and under successive administrations continued to devote most of its energies to the Shuttle program, no matter what damage would be done to space science and applications missions. NASA quit asking the question of which launch vehicle -- Shuttle or ELV -- would best achieve a particular mission's goals. To achieve, at least on paper, the high launch rate that would justify the costs of Shuttle development, all space programs (including military, commercial and scientific) were forced to employ Shuttle as the only carrier.

The process was completed with the well-known and incredibly unwise decision to launch the Galileo probe to Jupiter from

Shuttle. In a very eloquent statement to the House Committee on Science and Technology on July 21, 1986 Tom Donahue, Chairman of the Space Science Board of the National Academy of Sciences made some of these points most effectively:[3]

> . . . we urge that high priority be given to assessing the proper level of resources required for the nation's space program and the proper balance between manned and unmanned activities. This re-examination should assign to manned and unmanned systems and launch vehicles the roles that will permit each to serve the nation best, in contrast to the course we have been following for the past fifteen years.

*   *   *

> As a matter of highest priority in a re-energized national space program to which a realistic level of support is dedicated we strongly urge that the nation move rapidly toward the acquisition of a balanced fleet of launch vehicles that will provide assured access to space for all activities demanded by our national space program. The characteristics of these launch vehicles should be determined by the needs and requirements of all potential users, military, commercial and space science. We recommend that space transportation and launch systems be expeditiously acquired that will allow human resources to be used where they are needed and can be most effective and allow unmanned vehicles to be the carrier of choice for other missions.

The first lesson to be learned from the above is therefore quite clear:

NASA should recognize that manned exploration is not the only goal of the National space program. There exist other legitimate purposes for the use of space, and each user should be allowed to choose the most effective means to carry out his mission.

DIAGNOSTIC II

At the conclusion of his testimony Donahue made another important statement:

The objectives of the manned and unmanned elements of

the program should not be mixed in ways that reduce the effectiveness of either of them. To do so threatens the forfeiture of our scientific and technological leadership in space.

It is quite important to stress the very significant damage which is done to both human exploration and science and application activities when their objectives are confused. For space science the most direct damage done by the decision to force all payloads on the Shuttle was due to higher costs, long delays and in some cases outright cancellations. What is not sufficiently realized is the high cost in lowered scientific productivity which is experienced by projects which are carried out inappropriately.

A more subtle but equally tenacious effect is the distortion in scientific priorities which occurs when missions are carried out not on the basis of the best scientific opportunity but on the basis of the opportunities that exist to carry out science from the Space Shuttle (or the Space Station). The tragedy for science of the unused Shuttle payloads, which were developed but never flown, is not only that no science was produced, but also that those resources could have been used more effectively for other scientific missions of higher priority.

Let us now discuss the mixing of manned and unmanned programs with regard to reliability and choice of launcher.

Issues of Reliability

In the wake of the Challenger disaster there is even more concern at NASA and in Congress about the reliability of our space transportation. This concern, while entirely appropriate for activities which include human beings, is entirely inappropriate in so far as it concerns unmanned spacecraft and launches.

This is so because of the very high cost of achieving high launch reliability. While it is difficult (because of lack of data) to describe fully the relationship between reliability and cost, we have experience in the range of 90 to 95% reliability and we know that the relationship is very steep: The cost would become infinite as one approached a reliability of 100%. In fact we do not even understand how to reach 100% reliability nor could we ever know when we had reached it -- all we could ever know would be that we had not had a failure so far in our tests. (The small number of Shuttle flights means that statements about it being 99.999% reliable have no empirical basis.[4])

Thus different approaches are appropriate for manned and

94

unmanned flights. For manned flights it is appropriate to go to the highest practical reliability -- to be as safe as technology will allow.

On the other hand, what should be done for unmanned launches (i.e. for science and applications programs) is to maximize not the reliability of a single launch but the overall cost-effectiveness of the program. Depending on the value of the payload and the cost of higher reliability, a 90% reliable launcher might be more cost-effective than a 95% reliable one.

In sum, it is clear that any manned launch system (in which safety is paramount) is intrinsically more expensive than an unmanned one. Shuttle, therefore, never could have been a cheap launch system and it was a disservice to portray it as such. Further, it must be emphasized that the reliability needed in unmanned systems is only that which leads to minimum overall costs of achieving program goals. If this philosophy were fully adopted, a much more robust scientific program could be carried out at lower cost.

Choices of Launcher

The choices of a launcher for a particular scientific mission has many consequences which directly impinge on scientific productivity. I will discuss as an example, to illustrate the point, the choice by NASA to use the Space Shuttle to launch, service and reboost HST, which was made primarily for non-scientific reasons. This choice meant that HST had to operate in a low Earth orbit which could be reached by Shuttle. The intended benefits of the choice were: manned servicing in Shuttle orbit, heavy lift capability of the Shuttle, and safety (i.e. high reliability) of the Shuttle.

The actual disbenefits which were realized during the execution of the program were: reduced *system* reliability, unavailability of contingency servicing (because the Shuttle is unable to launch as often as anticipated), low observing efficiency (because the Earth obscures much of the sky), orbit risks (debris, glow, drag), higher costs (operations, man-rating, servicing), and complex planning and scheduling.

If the choice had been driven by scientific considerations, it is clear that a heavy lift expendable launch vehicle would have given substantial benefits: free orbit choice (which would have led to HST being in a geosynchronous orbit), reduced cost (lower complexity because it would not be serviceable on-orbit), enhanced science productivity (lower background, more continuous coverage), simpler operations (less complex scheduling, command and data reception) and finally increased programmatic reliability (the reduced operating and development costs would have made it possible to procure a backup for the same funds). There are further important scientific and engineering advantages to geosynchronous orbit which we can not fully describe here.

Suffice it to say that for scientific effectiveness the choice of mission profile, launch vehicle, orbit and reliability must be the subject of detailed engineering and cost tradeoff studies prior to selection. Such studies were never, to my knowledge, conducted on HST, or if they were conducted their results were not used.

DIAGNOSTIC III

There is a factor which needs further study, namely the high degree of technical engineering and managerial inefficiency which has become typical for civilian space missions in the last ten years.

In my opinion, this last aspect has been largely ignored by critics of the program. Yet, the result is there for all to see; namely, extremely large overruns, delays and failures.[5] Even those scholars who have experienced at first hand the problems in which some of the major NASA programs are entangled tend to accept the NASA explanation that all of this is the result of our unfortunate political system. In their view the inefficiencies of the program are the price which we must pay for big science in the shoddy system we have to work with. Based on first-hand experience, I hold the view that this general inefficiency is correlated with the source of the overruns, delays, and failures mentioned above, but did not cause them. Poor policy caused the problems, but while faultless execution might have mitigated poor strategic decisions, poor execution -- i.e. the general inefficiency -- further worsened the problem.[6]

To take a specific example, consider the history of the Hubble Space Telescope: No one forced the choice of Shuttle as its launch vehicle. No one forced the division of project management between two centers. No one forced the choice of contractors, the acceptance of their performance, the lack of system engineering, etc. What is clear is that the responsible officials did not have a technical understanding of the job at hand, could not manage it, relied on contractors, and neither could the contractors understand or manage the job. From this came the delays and overruns, and even worse the less than optimum design and performance. Granted that decisions dictated by politics may have affected performance, nevertheless no one prevented a good job from being done within the constraints. That is, political constraints have become an excuse for technical and management shortcomings.

What type of inefficiency exists and where does it show its major effect? The main factor in my opinion is the lack of NASA leadership in the planning and technical execution of the projects. NASA, after its high point of Apollo, has become more and more a contracting agency with much less in-house technical or managerial skill. Sustained inimical policies of successive administrations against the Federal civil service have resulted in the loss of the best technical and managerial people at the top of their profession. An increasingly old work force has become more and more bureaucratic and without the necessary skills to effectively direct the work of sub-contractors. Furthermore, demagogic attempts to reduce the "bureaucracy" by restricting hiring have resulted in the prevalent use of support contractors to carry out much of even that work which is ostensibly done "in-house." At Goddard Space Flight Center (GSFC), over 40% of the on-site manpower is provided in this manner. While judicious use of contractors may be extremely effective at times, we have reached the point when contractors now write the requirements for other contractors to execute. Contractors are used to manage the programs, produce reports and evaluate them.

Notwithstanding the above, NASA has insisted in retaining formal control of all its large projects, including the scientific ones, and has opposed attempts to create independent centers administered by university consortia to design and execute the science programs, an approach which is successfully employed by the Department of Energy (DOE) and the National Science Foundation (NSF). The only exception to the rule, the Jet Propulsion Laboratory, has been turned almost completely into a wholly-owned subsidiary, which still retains technical competence but whose efficiency is not much higher than the norm for a contractor under management by a NASA center.

Such a hands-on management approach, of which NASA is very proud, might have had some justification at the beginning of the space program when space technology was being developed. The situation is quite different today -- most of the competence in this field resides outside NASA.

There have been cases in which missions in trouble have been rescued by the contractor. That is, NASA *de facto* surrendered control and the contractor was able to take action to accomplish the mission, although sometimes at high cost. This is not good practice because costs tend to escalate; the contractor may have different priorities; and it is an abdication of responsibility. While this practice may suffice for small missions it will not work acceptably for large ones; neither NASA nor the contractors have the *scientific* and systems engineering expertise to properly design large, sophisticated scientific missions. In sum, NASA's current approach is to attempt to manage all aspects of mission development whether it has the competence or not.

The effects of the current approach are quite clear and fatal:

-- Space science programs, especially the most sophisticated, are not designed at the outset on the basis of a clear technical approach, an overall architecture, or clear lines of responsibility and management.

-- Technical choices submitted by the contractors (who will build the mission hardware) are decided without sufficient in-depth evaluation or trade-off. When, later in the program, it is discovered that the initial choice was wrong, large delays and expenditures ensue, and these often affect the entire program. .

-- Often the academic and industrial groups involved in a program agree to conduct it in a manner dictated by NASA because the immediate program is seen as the only game in town. For this same reason, those in the best position to criticize NASA tend to be silent. The advisory committees also are captive of the agency: While they are frequently asked to comment about specific choices of payloads or mission, they are seldom, if ever, allowed to question the wisdom of the overall NASA approach. The protests that were raised by concerned scientists regarding the Shuttle program at its inception were largely ignored and similar issues now being raised regarding the Space Station are almost contemptuously brushed aside.

-- Program management responsibilities are split among NASA centers on the basis of a spoils system rather than effectiveness. The centers themselves often do not have the competence for systems engineering and management of the programs.

-- The contractors respond to NASA solicitations with a "buy-in" price designed for presentation to Congress and with an unrealistic relationship to performance goals and schedule. After the agency is fully committed to a program even the most conservative (i.e. highest) initial estimates are exceeded. NASA is impotent to control these escalating costs. Furthermore, most of the large aerospace contractors are accustomed to work in a non-competitive captive market whose efficiency is set by the standards of the Department of Defense (DOD).

My own experience is that the difference in cost in hardware and software between programs run in this manner and those under the direct control of dedicated, competent scientists, engineers and managers can be very large.

In short, my view is that integrity and technical competence must be restored to the NASA program both in conception and in execution if we are to realize the enormous potential for achievement still present in this Nation. In my opinion, fundamental reform cannot long be postponed because of the present and ever worsening "generation gap" of experience in space technology and space sciences.[7] If we do not move quickly, we may face a very long period of recovery or we may never recapture a leading position in space science.

SPECIFIC SUGGESTIONS FOR RECOVERY

It is quite obvious that science and technology play an important part in numerous areas of national interest ranging from defense and national prestige to industrial competitiveness. Therefore, it is remarkable that the Presidential appointees to key positions in national scientific establishments are not subject to the same kind of careful review as are other Presidential appointees. Although the competent committees of the Senate do indeed review the qualifications of appointees such as the Director of NSF, the Administrator of NASA, and the Secretary of Defense, as well as the qualifications for some appointees to lower level positions within these agencies, from the point of view of science and technology this review is relatively perfunctory in that it does not involve professional scientists, the professional societies, or the National Academy of Sciences or of Engineering in the same manner as, for instance, the American Bar Association is involved in commenting on judicial appointments. The appointment of a scientific advisor to the President does not require the advice and consent of the Senate. In the absence of a single cabinet-level appointment of a scientist to direct the national research effort which would require such approval (or alternatively the reconstitution of President's Science Advisory

Committee), it is obviously of great interest to insure that these other appointments go to persons who can assume leadership in these key areas and particularly in the direction of our space program.

Specific suggestions for improving the conduct of our space exploration and space science efforts are discussed below.

Manned Exploration

The manned exploration effort of NASA has been plagued in the last several years by the lack of a long term plan which establishes goals broadly supported by the administration and Congress. Such a goal might, for example, include the establishment of a small permanent colony on the Moon or Mars. The nature of the goals should be such that we could hope to reach them within 50 years. The time for the achievement of substantial steps along this path could be determined and either shortened or prolonged according to a budget-constrained, step-by-step program which would permit us to go from where we are today to where we want to be.

In this light, one would ask questions such as - where does the current transportation system fit into the overall plan and where does the Space Station fit?

Space Station in itself is not a goal. Goals cannot be centered on a piece of hardware. Goals must express a program or a mission which specific hardware is then designed to execute. The fit should not only be a tenuous marketing convenience but a real technical congruence so that the designs, hardware and procedures which are adopted today are part of an overall design which will evolve to meet the requirements of tomorrow. From this point of view, the current Space Station design could be improved to optimize its role in the long term program.

The main suggestions, therefore, for strengthening the exploratory manned program would be to decide on a goal and then develop a rational plan to achieve that goal. Scientific advisory bodies such as the Space Science Board of the NAS could play a more supportive role in a rigorous process of selecting targets for human exploration. They could then help define the scientific precursory requirements and the strategy to be adopted in acquiring the necessary knowledge. These precursor requirements could include:

-- medical knowledge of human response to the space environment;

-- data from exploratory and reconnaissance robotic missions; and

-- technological skills required to utilize *in situ* materials (which may encompass metallurgy, chemistry, energy sources, etc.).

Given that the Space Station will be implemented, then the Space Science Board should assess the role Station should play in implementing the strategy and how it should be designed to fulfill this role. One can anticipate that the primary objective for Station will be addressing some of the scientific precursor requirements outlined above: Accordingly, the Space Station should be optimized to carry out these tasks.

Given that Space Station resources will be at a premium, secondary uses of the Space Station (which would include the conduct of other science which does not uniquely require the Station or manned involvement) should be prioritized. This prioritization should be carried out only after studies of scientific productivity versus total costs, considering trade-offs among different alternatives for each proposed project.

The management of the human exploration program in general, or of the Space Station program in particular, should not extend to or impact scientific missions for which there is no rational connection to manned missions. As an example, the Polar Platform Program (of remote sensing of the Earth) shares neither the launches nor the orbit of the Space Station. Manned involvement in the execution of that program has no justification. Given the great importance of the Polar Platform in the NASA program and indeed to the Earth and all mankind, it should be carried out in the most effective manner.

Space Science Program

As to the space science program, it has a well-studied set of scientific goals and objectives, both short and long range. However, the program could not be carried out in the past because of a number of financial and technical constraints which have been imposed upon it by NASA management in the mistaken belief that they would benefit the manned program. A large number of experiments have been developed and brought to flight readiness to take advantage of the Shuttle flight opportunities and have been cancelled when the flights did not materialize.[8] This represents money irretrievably lost from space science. Several important scientific missions are waiting on the ground for flight opportunities. Finally, the science which was being done was the best that could be done from the Shuttle, not the best science that could be done.

Similar negative effects can be expected by coupling the space science program too tightly to the future Space Station program. Should this negative influence be removed and the science programs allowed to use mainly Expendable Launch Vehicles (ELVs), the current expenditure in the space sciences would be sufficient, with modest augmentation, to carry out an extensive and extremely productive space science program. Therefore, the main requirements for space science are independence from the exploratory manned programs of NASA and a steady budgetary commitment.

The current costs of space science missions have become so large that only a small fraction of the desirable missions can be carried out within the current budgetary constraints. This cost increase has been due to a set of circumstances only partly outside of NASA's control. Inflation is often mentioned as having taken its toll on the costs of producing high technology instrumentation although the cost of high technology equipment is steadily decreasing in the commercial sector. The bulk of the increase in costs is due, in my opinion, to inappropriate management of scientific space ventures and to an inappropriate set of relationships among the three main actors in this field: NASA and its Centers, industrial contractors, and academic research institutions. The management approach as well as the institutional relationships between these three components of the national space program should be restructured in order to substantially increase the efficiency with which space ventures and particularly space science can be carried out. This will not be easy.

It will also be difficult to redefine the role of NASA centers because of political considerations and the constraints of the civil service system although it is clear in many instances that management of programs by centers causes inefficiencies. For many scientific missions a delegation of responsibility to a competent scientific consortium and subcontracting by the consortium to industry would be much more effective.

However, NASA centers will continue to be involved both in manned programs and in those activities in the science program that cut across disciplines. Therefore, it is imperative that the management, engineering, and technical competence of these centers be upgraded. A possible solution would be the transformation of these centers into government-owned contractor-operated centers such as the Applied Physics Laboratory or the Lincoln Laboratories, etc., which would no longer be subject to Civil Service regulations.

It is my opinion that the adoption of these suggestions could greatly enhance our competitive posture with respect to the USSR, Japan and Europe. While the need for such reforms may have been apparent for some time, deeply entrenched interests in the bureaucracy and in industry may delay their acceptance. What would insure their serious consideration might be the formation of a broad consensus in the scientific and technical community that such changes are required; the determination of the ways and means to bring such changes about by students of science policy; and, finally and most importantly, actual perception by the Executive branch that a crisis exists in the physical sciences and more particularly in space ventures and that fundamental reforms are urgently required.

NOTES

1. NASA Advisory Council, Space and Earth Science Advisory Committee, *The Crisis in Space and Earth Science* (Washington, D.C.: NASA, 1986).

2. W. Hively, "A Resurgent NASA Woos Scientists Back to the Space Program" *American Scientist 77*, March-April 1989, p. 132. Hively reports a presentation by Lennard Fisk, NASA Assistant Administrator for Space Science and Applications, at which he said NASA has idled about a million pounds of payload since the Challenger accident.

3. U.S. House of Representatives, Committee on Science and Technology, *Assured Access to Space: 1986*, Hearings, 99th Congress, No. 164 (Washington, D.C.: U.S.G.P.O., 1986).

4. Testimony by Dr. Milton Silveira of NASA is that NASA's design objective for the Shuttle was 1 failure in 100,000. See U.S. House of Representatives, Committee on Science and Technology, *Review of RTG Utilization in Space Missions*, Hearing, 99th Congress, No. 97 (Washington, D.C.: U.S.G.P.O., 1986), p. 39.

5. (a) Space Exploration/Cost, Schedule, and Performance of NASA's Galileo Mission to Jupiter, GAO/NSIAD-88-138FS. (b) Space Exploration/NASA's Deep Space Missions are Experiencing Long Delays, GAO/NSIAD-88-128BR. (c) Space Exploration/Cost, Schedule, and Performance of NASA's Magellan Mission to Venus, GAO/NSIAD-88-130FS. (d) Space Exploration/Cost, Schedule, and Performance of NASA's Ulysses

Mission to the Sun, GAO/NSIAD-88-129FS. All U.S. General Accounting Office, May, 1988, Washington, D.C.

6. Stuart Diamond, "NASA Wasted Billions, Federal Audits Disclose," *New York Times*, April 23, 1986, p. 1.

7. By "generation gap" I refer to the fact that the generation of early experimental physicists such as Jim Van Allen, Ed Stone, Frank McDonald, Herb Friedman and myself are retiring. These people could design rockets, spacecraft, missions, and experiments, analyze data, manage groups, etc. Of the scientists now in their 40s very few have had the opportunity to do things on their own. Who are the young to learn from?

8. The exact number of such experiments is difficult to know. It was originally reported in briefings as being around 50, but it now appears that some of these will be postponed rather than cancelled.

Chapter 6

CIVILIAN SPACE APPLICATIONS:
THE PRIVATIZATION BATTLEGROUND

Marcia S. Smith[1]

IS IT PROGRESS IF A CANNIBAL USES A FORK?

STANISLAW J. LEC

When space was new and emotions ran high about the potential of space technology for improving everyday life, the question of who was going to develop that technology had an easy answer: NASA. Those days are long since past, and to many it seems that no one is now "in charge" of developing new technologies for space applications or ensuring that the mature programs survive. The proliferation of government agencies involved in civilian space has muddied the waters in terms of deciding policy for space applications. Coupled with the Reagan Administration's emphasis on turning government programs over to the private sector, many areas of space applications seem to have become foundlings bouncing between orphanage and foster home.

The focus of this paper is intentionally limited to three areas of civilian space applications: communications, land remote sensing, and weather.[2] For these areas, the issues have several facets. Are the technologies mature enough that the private sector should take charge of developing more advanced systems? If the private sector refuses, should the country abandon those technologies; that is, should the future of space applications "sink or swim" on the private sector's willingness to take them over? Or do these technologies play a crucial role in the overall technological competitiveness of the country and therefore deserve taxpayer support? If the government is to play a role, what agency should be responsible?

PRIVATE SECTOR VERSUS GOVERNMENT SUPPORT

The three types of applications programs covered here have unique histories following initial development by NASA. Communications satellites were quickly spun off to the private sector, although NASA remained active in research and development until 1973. A six year period followed in which the private sector was expected to take responsibility for developing new technologies, and when it did not, NASA reentered the research and development area in 1979. Operation of land remote sensing satellites (the Landsat program) was transferred to another government agency, the National Oceanic and Atmospheric Administration (NOAA, part of the Department of Commerce), and then to the private sector in 1985, with NASA retaining primary responsibility for research and development. Weather satellites were transferred to NOAA, which still operates them today and has assumed responsibility for research and development as well.

Communications Satellites

U.S. government investment in communications satellite research in the earliest days of the space program not only allowed development of increasingly sophisticated satellites for the United States, but for the rest of the free world. Through the creation of Intelsat, world-wide communications became a reality and U.S. satellite manufacturing companies profited.[3] Today, the United States continues to be the world leader in manufacturing communications satellites, but European industry has become very strong in this area and Japan will probably pose a competitive threat in the future. New technologies to permit satellites to operate at higher frequencies (outside the increasingly congested bands in common use today), and enable inter-satellite links and on-board processing, appear to be the wave of the future. The question can reasonably be asked: If a customer wants these new technologies, why shouldn't the communications satellite industry pay for developing them and pass the cost along to the client? If industry is not willing to assume this responsibility and/or customers are not willing to bear the costs, why should the government pay for them?

This argument has been at the heart of the debate over the Advanced Communications Technology Satellite (ACTS) which continues its uncertain life due to Congressional insistence that the government develop advanced communications satellite technology to ensure continued U.S. preeminence in this highly competitive market area. After NASA terminated its communications satellite research and development program in 1973, the private sector did not come forward to fill the void. Concerned that the United States would lose its competitive advantage, NASA resumed research and development in 1979. The program that ultimately become known as ACTS was seen as a novel method of government-industry space cooperation where each side contributes to the program. The contractor building the satellite and the groups that plan to perform experiments using it agreed to put up approximately twenty percent of the program costs ($100 million of a $450 million program).[4]

The tumultuous history of the ACTS program is described elsewhere, and each year the drama replays itself.[5] The salient issue has been whether the U.S. government deems these new technologies so important to the economic competitiveness of the U.S. communication satellite industry that government investment is warranted. The Reagan Administration repeatedly said no and there apparently is no change of view in the Bush Administration; the Congress says yes, each year reinstating the program after the Administration zeroes the funding.

When the prospect of terminating ACTS first arose, the vast majority of private sector representatives argued that research and development was too expensive for them to pursue alone.[6] They insisted that if the government would not step up to its responsibility in this area, they would simply buy the new technology satellites from other countries. This was a surprising attitude from an industry that presumably would have been hurt by foreign encroachment; perhaps the private sector simply assumed that the government would feel forced to perform the research and development and relieve them of the burden.[7] The operative point is that whether or not industry *should* have assumed the research and development responsibility, it did not, except to the extent it is contributing to ACTS. Admittedly the ACTS program has been less than trouble-free since the signing of the contract,[8] but government/industry partnerships may be a model for other areas of space applications technology development.

Land Remote Sensing (LANDSAT)

The perennial tug of war between the Administration and Congress over ACTS has earned it the distinction of being a sad chapter in the history of the development of space applications, but it pales in comparison to the problems encountered by the Landsat program. The Government has devoted so much energy to the question of who should be responsible for Landsat, that it seems to have lost sight of the crucial issue of the need for the system both to satisfy U.S. government data requirements and to compete with other countries. The very existence of the system today is in jeopardy because of the policy dispute.

The issue with ACTS is who should be responsible for advanced research and development; for Landsat, that issue is coupled with a larger question of who should operate the system. Communications satellites could be spun off to the private sector for operation early in their history because there was a clear market for the product; this is not the case for land remote sensing satellites. Seventeen years after the first Landsat was launched, there still does not appear to be a sufficient market to support a totally private company.

Details about the road to privatization of Landsat can be found in a wealth of congressional hearings beginning as early as 1973 and continuing today.[9] Briefly, the satellites were developed by NASA and declared "operational" in 1979. Subsequently they were turned over to NOAA with the eventual goal of private sector operation after 10 years. The Reagan Administration chose to accelerate that schedule, and following enactment of the 1984 Land Remote Sensing Commercialization Act (the Landsat Act, P.L. 98-365), operation of the Landsat system was turned over to EOSAT, a private company selected through a competitive bidding process.[10] The Administration agreed to provide $250 million over five years to EOSAT, but after the first installment, tried to renege on its promises. Congress insisted that the Administration meet its obligations, and Landsat became caught in the crossfire. The original contract called for EOSAT to develop two new spacecraft (Landsat 6 and 7), and operate Landsat 4 and 5, which remain in orbit, at government expense.

Today, NOAA and EOSAT are curtailing most Landsat 4 and 5 operations because of insufficient funding, and the contract has been modified so that only one follow-on satellite will be built. The Administration's position is that if EOSAT fails, then so does the Landsat system; the government will not build any more

Landsats. This "sink or swim" approach is surprising considering the government's own needs for Landsat data, as expressed time and again in congressional hearings by the Departments of Agriculture, Interior and Defense.[11] The never ending argument that if the user agencies need Landsat data then they should pay for the system has overshadowed the more important point that *someone* needs to ensure that the system survives. The user agencies assert that the President assigned responsibility for Landsat to the Department of Commerce; the Department of Commerce says the users should pay at least part of the bill and that it has other funding priorities that must be met. Meanwhile, the system is dying.

EOSAT has its strong critics, but there is no question that the basic problem has been the Administration's change of heart about providing EOSAT the promised subsidies. EOSAT understandably complains that it cannot be expected to develop a market for Landsat data when there is no guarantee that there will be a Landsat system, and it cannot make that guarantee without the promised government support.

Land remote sensing satellites are valuable assets, as evidenced not only by the multitude of uses to which the data are put, but the fact that France and the Soviet Union have jumped on the bandwagon with their own systems.[12] Japan and the European Space Agency may enter the market when their land remote sensing systems are launched in the next few years. France and the Soviet Union have the benefit of strong government support either directly or indirectly, unlike EOSAT which is expected to fend for itself amidst policy turmoil. Perhaps the market for remote sensing data will never grow to the point where EOSAT can make sufficient profit to be completely independent of the government. This does not mean that the United States should abandon Landsat, or that the program should be taken back into the protective arms of the Government. The solution may be what has become a pejorative term in recent years: subsidies. Though hardly a panacea, government subsidies can be a useful compromise between government operation of the system, and private operation under the "sink or swim" approach.

Responsibility for research and development on new land remote sensing instruments is shared by EOSAT and NASA (which is directed by the Landsat Act to continue and enhance remote sensing research and development programs). EOSAT clearly will develop new sensors only where it would be profitable, and NASA's efforts are subject to severe budget constraints and it is extremely difficult to identify specific NASA programs for land remote sensing R&D. NASA is not planning to build any more Landsat-type satellites in any case.

The important question is whether U.S. satellites will be able to keep pace with developments in other countries. The current uncertainty about whether the next Landsat will have 5 meter resolution is a case in point.[13] One segment of the user community, the media, has expressed some interest in a satellite providing this level of detail, but apparently it is insufficient to convince EOSAT to take the risk of developing this new sensor, and there is no indication that NASA plans to develop a 5 meter sensor either.[14] Since 5 meter data are already available from the Soviet Union, the United States could lose a developing market. Many in the space community feel that land remote sensing R&D has slipped through the cracks, and with it, this country's preeminence in the field.

As noted, EOSAT is about to stop most operations of Landsat 4 and 5 for lack of funds, and the new Landsat 6 will not be launched until the early 1990s. It seems ironic that the country that pioneered the development of land remote sensing satellites may soon have to rely on foreign countries to provide that very data.[15]

Weather Satellites

Apparently because weather forecasting is an essential element of everyday life and bears an important relationship to national defense (although DOD has its own system), NOAA's weather satellites were exempted from the privatization drive.[16] The prominent issue involving weather satellites in recent years has been how many satellites should be in orbit at one time, not who should perform advanced research and development or operate the satellites. In this cost conscious era, the Administration has argued that only one polar-orbiting weather satellite is necessary. Recent launch vehicle and satellite failures underscore the risks associated with this approach.

However, the questions of R&D and operational responsibility do warrant attention. NASA has broad plans to develop earth observing sensors, especially for the polar platform being developed as part of the Space Station program.[17] NOAA, however, is responsible for new weather satellite sensors, identifying the need for new instruments and then contracting for the work to be done. NOAA was made responsible for weather satellite R&D chiefly because of NASA budgetary constraints, but it seems reasonable to ask why centralization of such activities in NASA would not be a better course since it already has responsibility for R&D in the other earth observing disciplines. An integrated approach to R&D seems preferable, especially as in the future multiple sensors may be integrated onto a single platform.

A similar argument could be made for operations. Some observers argue that, like land remote sensing, weather satellites should be operated by EOSAT.[18] Presumably, the government itself would then become the major customer for the data, essentially guaranteeing a market. If the government is willing to make purchase guarantees or otherwise show willingness to step in and provide support if EOSAT falters, there seems little reason not to spin weather satellites off to the private sector.[19] A change in policy would be required, however, since commercialization of weather satellites was specifically prohibited in the Landsat Act. Agreements presumably could be formulated to rectify Congressional concern by giving the government unrestricted use of the data once it was purchased from EOSAT (or another private company). Thus, all users (domestic and international) who currently receive free weather data from the U.S. Government would continue to do so.

For the immediate future, though, it appears that the government will continue to operate the weather satellites. There are three options to accomplish this goal: continue operations through NOAA as part of the Department of Commerce; establish NOAA as a separate agency; or bring NOAA's satellite operations into NASA in order to centralize all space operations in a single agency. The first option would be appealing to those who feel that the current situation is working satisfactorily. But there have been arguments for many years that as part of the Department of Commerce, NOAA is treated as a poor cousin, especially when difficult budget choices have to be made. Efforts to generate support for establishing NOAA as a separate agency, however, have failed to succeed so far. The third option, bringing NOAA's satellite operations into NASA, is based on the theory that centralization of responsibility and authority could eliminate disarray and duplication. Although this option would have to be rigorously studied, it does warrant consideration.

WHO SHOULD BE IN CHARGE?

Although studies have shown that the greatest impact on economic competitiveness is from R&D performed by industry itself, not government,[20] if industry will not make that investment, the importance of governmental programs grow. This has been the case for communications satellites and may become true for land remote sensing if EOSAT fails. Given this reality, the Government needs to reassess investment in new space applications technologies, as well as its responsibility for operating systems that the private sector will not take over, or fails to successfully privatize.

Where government is responsible for developing new technologies, the question arises as to how to marry user needs with the development of technologies so advanced that they strain the user community's ability to forecast its future needs. Should the scientists and engineers performing research and development closely listen to the users when developing new technologies? Of course. Have they in the past? Not always. Does this mean they are incapable of taking user needs into consideration? Certainly not. Should research and development be performed only for those new technologies that have an identifiable existing user base? No, since a major aspect of performing research and development is to push the technological frontier. Both user-identified and breakthrough technologies need to be developed.

These are questions of program management as much as policy. When a government agency takes the responsibility for research and development, it clearly must be done in close cooperation with the user community (inside and outside the government) and, where possible, the satellite manufacturing industry in government-industry partnerships. If no industry partner can be found, however, there is a strong argument that the government must be prepared to proceed alone rather than risk losing technological leadership and, with it, economic competitiveness.

Another important point is that government responsibility for a technology or a system should not end at some arbitrary pronouncement of "operational" status.[21] While every effort should be made to encourage privatization of systems, the ultimate need for the systems should not be lost in the cacophony of arguments over who should be in charge of what. Subsidizing interested private sector parties, at least through the initial rough years and perhaps longer if necessary, may be a reasonable alternative.

Where government operation is required, centralization of responsibility could be an attractive choice. Today, government civilian space operations are split between NASA (the shuttle, procurement of other launch vehicles/services, and tracking and data functions) and NOAA (weather satellites and oversight of the EOSAT contract). Bringing NOAA's satellite operations into NASA might create efficiencies in the bureaucratic structure needed to support space programs, and close cooperation between R&D activities such as the Earth Observing System (see note 16) and operational activities could benefit both.

The user community would undoubtedly be concerned that if weather satellites, for example, were put back in NASA's hands, technological advances might be pursued at the expense of getting today's job done in terms of weather forecasting. One solution would be to transfer the individuals who operate the programs at NOAA to NASA and put them in overall charge of the program. Several high level NOAA satellite managers began their careers with NASA so there is ample precedent for such transfers. They could benefit from close interaction with those developing new technologies, but would bring their experience in meeting day to day requirements. NASA's main problem in assuming such a role would be budgetary, but centralizing responsibility might lead to less duplication of bureaucracies and thus lead to cost savings for the government as a whole.

In recent years, the debate over whether NASA is strictly a research and development agency, not an operational one, has repeatedly surfaced. The 1958 National Aeronautics and Space Act which created NASA leaves ample room for interpretation, and in any case, NASA's mandate needs to be debated in today's reality, not that of 1958. Thus the question is whether NASA *should* be involved only in research and development, or if it has a proper role in operating space systems.

There is always the danger that an agency overwhelmed by operational requirements might be tempted to raid the resources available for research and development, thus threatening innovative science and applications programs. However, this is a problem of management and funding, not of mandate. Some have suggested that for the shuttle program an agency within an agency be created along the lines of the Tennessee Valley Authority model, so that operations funding would be strictly separated from research and development. This approach could be considered for space operations generally.

CONCLUSION

If the United States wants to maintain a strong competitive posture in an increasingly technologically sophisticated world, the Government has a vital interest in supporting new technologies. As has been demonstrated with the ACTS program, the private sector cannot always be depended upon to push new technological frontiers even for mature systems like communications satellites. In some cases the government may have to act alone, but in others, government-industry partnerships can be pursued, as was done for ACTS. Similarly, the government has a responsibility for mature space applications programs, especially where the government itself is a major user of the product. While every effort should be made to turn applications programs over to the private sector, the current "sink or swim" approach, which risks the continued existence of programs like Landsat, seems a perilous course. In some cases, the government may actually have to resume operation of systems if they are to survive, but subsidies could be a preferable alternative.

Considering the wide variety of options available for R&D and operation of space applications programs, it is bewildering that the United States now finds itself in the position of fighting to maintain leadership in technologies that it pioneered. As with most areas of space policy, the ultimate requirement is for strong leadership first in setting policy, and then implementing it in a consistent manner. This will be the ultimate challenge for the Bush Administration.

NOTES

1. Marcia Smith is a Specialist in Aerospace Policy for the Congressional Research Service, a department of the Library of Congress, Washington, D.C. The views expressed here do not necessarily represent those of CRS or the Library of Congress.

2. The reader should note, however, that the space applications umbrella extends to other types of remote sensing and atmospheric measurements, including projects such as the Earth Observing System, the Upper Atmosphere Research Satellite, and the Ocean Topography Experiment, as well as microgravity materials processing. Also, there are government-funded and operated military space applications programs.

3. Intelsat is the International Telecommunications Satellite Organization which currently has 114 member countries. The U.S. representative to Intelsat is Comsat, the Communications Satellite Corp.

4. RCA was selected as the contractor and it was later bought by General Electric.

5. See, for example: Marcia S. Smith, NASA's Advanced Communications Satellite Technology Program (ACTS) Program in Light of the Hughes Filing (Washington, D.C.: Congressional Research Service, Library of Congress, March 2, 1984).

6. The exception was Hughes Aircraft, which stated that it would accept the responsibility, but Congress was concerned about the consequences if Hughes later changed its mind.

7. Through the MILSTAR program, the government was paying for advanced communications satellite R&D in any case, but it is specially suited for military applications, not commercial.

8. TRW, one of the subcontractors, was dismissed from the program in 1988 because of substantial cost overruns.

9. Historical reviews are contained in: (1) U.S. Congress. House. Committee on Science and Technology. United States Civilian Space Programs, Volume II. Prepared by the Congressional Research Service. (Washington, D.C.: U.S. Government Printing Office, May 1983), chapter 5. (2) U.S. Congress. House. Committee on Science and Technology. Commercialization of Land and Weather Satellites. Prepared by the Congressional Research Service. (Washington, D.C.: U.S. Government Printing Office, June 1983). For more recent information, see: Marcia S. Smith, Privatization of the Landsat Remote Sensing Satellite System: Current Issues (Congressional Research Service, Library of Congress, (Washington, D.C.: June 5, 1987, CRS Report 87-477 SPR).

10. EOSAT is a partnership of Hughes Aircraft (now part of General Motors) and RCA (now owned by General Electric).

11. Most recently in 1987. See: U.S. Congress. House Committee on Science, Space and Technology. The Future of the Landsat System. Hearings, March 31, April 2, 1987. 100th Congress, 1st session. (Washington, D.C.: U.S. Government Printing Office, 1987).

12. Typical uses include land use planning, crop forecasting, and pollution monitoring.

13. Though admittedly an oversimplified definition, "resolution" is the ability to "see" an object on the ground, so a sensor with 5 meter resolution would be able to discern features 5 meters or more in diameter. Landsat 4 and 5 have 30 meter resolution. The French SPOT satellite has either 10 or 20 meter resolution (black and white, and color, respectively).

14. There are restrictions on what the Soviets make available, however. They will only sell data about the customer's country, so a U.S. company could not obtain data on Argentina, for example.

15. In early 1989, NOAA began exploratory talks with the French space agency CNES about merging Landsat and the French SPOT system. How far the talks will go, and what reaction Congress would have to an actual proposal like this, is extremely unclear.

16. The Administration did, in fact, propose commercializing weather satellites, but Congress specifically and emphatically prohibited it in the Landsat Act.

17. A "platform" is a large spacecraft that can serve as home to a large number of diverse sensors, rather than a single satellite devoted to a particular purpose. A platform might have sensors for weather, land remote sensing, and ocean sensing, for example. "Polar" refers to an orbit that circles the Earth's poles (as opposed to an equatorial orbit, for example). NASA, in cooperation with Europe and Japan, plans to build an Earth Observing System to study the entire globe using polar platforms as part of Mission to Planet Earth.

18. John McElroy, Dean of Engineering at the University of Texas at Arlington and former Assistant Administrator for Satellites at the Department of Commerce (in charge of Landsat and the weather satellites), is a proponent of this approach. He suggests that EOSAT could operate the weather satellites, and become the U.S. representative to an international organization created along the lines of Intelsat for earth observation data.

19. Some would argue that such guarantees would be a subsidy, although others would point out that it would be money the government would have to spend in any case.

20. Lennard G. Kruger, et al., Commercialization of Technology and Issues in the Competitiveness of Selected U.S. Industries: Semiconductors, Biotechnology, and Superconductors (Washington, D.C.: Congressional Research Service, Library of Congress, Revised August 1, 1988, CRS Report 99-486 SPR).

21. It is often argued that "operational" status is determined more by political than technical factors.

Chapter 7

INFRASTRUCTURES: THE HARDWARE, THE FIRMWARE, AND THE SOFTWARE

M. Mitchell Waldrop

To a man with a hammer, everything looks like a nail.

This chapter addresses three fundamental questions: What is space infrastructure? What are space operations? And why are they important to a reconsideration of space policy?

On one level these questions appear easy to answer. Infrastructure is hardware -- launch pads, Shuttles, Space Stations, and Tracking and Data Relay Satellites. In short, all the material and equipment that we use to get things done in space. Operations, on the other hand, are all the things we have to do to run the hardware. They are important because it seems inevitable that infrastructure and operations are going to dominate NASA's budget for as long as any one can foresee -- which means that what is probably *the* fundamental space policy problem is only going to get worse and worse: namely, that the cost of building and maintaining all the hardware makes it harder and harder to actually do anything with it, i.e. science or applications.

Barring some kind of revolution in the funding climate, fresh solutions to this problem are needed but lacking. A broader perspective, then, may generate some fresh insight.

This chapter does not focus on hardware, i.e. Space Stations, Orbital Transfer Vehicles, Orbital Maneuvering Vehicles, Advanced Launch Systems (OTV's, OMV's, ALS's), etc. The reasoning for this is that there is a whole different level of infrastructure that comes into play before hardware is relevant. One can think of this as "firmware." For example:

Institutional Infrastructure -- This refers to the way people are organized to get things done; how responsibilities for operations are divided up; technology development, scientific research, and regulation.   Included   in   this   category   are   NASA,   DOD, Commerce, Transportation, universities that do research, and the various aerospace companies.

Decision-Making Infrastructure -- This means the framework for making   decisions.   Included   are   SIG-Space,   the   various congressional committees, and the multitudinous advisory groups. An example of decision-making infrastructure is the way that a rather   arbitrary   historical   process   has   put   the   NASA appropriations budget under the control of the HUD-Independent Agencies subcommittees -- which means that, when push comes to shove, space science and Space Stations have to fight it out against low-income housing and the environment, instead of, for example, the B1 bomber.

Financial Infrastructure -- This encompasses various sources for funding space activities, from the U.S. Treasury to the venture capital markets.

The Political Infrastructure -- This is composed of the groups that have a stake in the space program, and all the mechanisms they use for articulating their demands.   These range from the Space Science Working Group to the L5 Society to the aerospace lobby.

This is probably not an exhaustive list, and the examples are certainly not mutually exclusive.   Quite the opposite: they're incestuous. They blend, and overlap, and intertwine. The point is that this kind of firmware infrastructure is at least as important for getting things done as the hardware. Furthermore, it is just as much a human construct as any piece of hardware, and deserves just as much careful thought in its design -- preferably before developing a lot of new hardware. The question is whether NASA and the other institutions built for the space program as it was in the 1960s are really still suited for the space program as it is now.

A partial answer lies in an examination of three of the most basic truisms about infrastructure.

TRUISM #1: INFRASTRUCTURE IS A SET OF TOOLS, A MEANS TO AN END

This may have been repeated so often that its message is dulled. But it is still true, and it illuminates the reasons why our struggles with space policy seem to have mired us in a swamp. The reason is that the country as a whole can't seem to agree on why it wants to have a space program. Arguments over all the various infrastructure issues -- the Space Station, Industrial Space Facilities, next-generation launch systems, and so forth -- are really just surrogates for the real arguments. Furthermore, the real arguments are rarely about anything so crisp and well-defined as a "goal." In fact, the usual prescription for what ails the space program -- give NASA a goal such as a manned mission to Mars -- may not settle anything.

Consider that a goal by itself is little more than a label, a slogan. But what really drives a space program (or any other human activity, for that matter) is what might be called the "cognitive" infrastructure: the set of mental models, tacit assumptions, prejudices, and implicit agendas that govern people's perception of what space is and what the space program is all about. Alongside hardware and firmware, this can be thought of as "software."

To find an example of this, look back at the Sputnik and Apollo eras, perhaps the last time the U.S. had a national consensus on space. At the time it seemed very clear to everyone what space was: namely, a frontier. After all, just getting into space was a heroic achievement. Space flight was at the cutting edge of technology, enormously difficult, enormously expensive, and something only governments could afford -- and only superpower governments at that. Space, in short, was government's "turf."

From that, given the state of the Cold War at the time, it was a short step to a national consensus on what the space program was all about: namely, national security and national prowess. The U.S. had to seize the high ground and restore national pride, beating the Russians no matter what it cost. Thus, nearly anything was justified if it helped the U.S. get ahead in the space race.

What crystallized out of that perception? First, the space side of the aerospace industry, which was building all kinds of rockets and ballistic missiles for the Pentagon. Second, on the civilian side there was NASA -- the centers, the launch facilities at the Cape, the Saturn rockets, and a whole cadre of engineers and technicians, all focused on that one goal of getting men to the moon and back.

The Apollo program was a glorious adventure, one that the country can deservedly be proud of. But in hindsight, the Apollo program had some consequences that were not so nice, consequences that need to be kept clearly in mind at a time when some people are calling for a massive effort to put humans on Mars. For example:

-- Because it was a crash program, Apollo had a lot of opportunity costs. In hardware terms we can classify those costs as sins of commission, in that the program left us with some expensive hardware (i.e. the lunar module) that could not be used for anything else; and sins of omission, in that there were alternative technologies, such as techniques for earth orbit rendezvous and in-orbit assembly, that couldn't be pursued even though they might have been useful for a lot of things later.

-- Together with Vietnam and a certain anti-technology mood in general, the Apollo program helped push the pendulum of public opinion back against technology and space, where it froze in place for nearly a decade. Space was clearly still a frontier. But by the early 1970s there was a widespread perception that the race with the Russians was over. Therefore, why keep running it?

The result was a general decline of and skepticism toward the space program; the rusting Saturn 5 out on the lawn at Kennedy; OMB's very successful efforts to slash the NASA budget during the 1970s; Carter's nearly successful attempt to kill the Shuttle program in 1977; widespread cynicism in the 1980s that the Shuttle and/or the Space Station are really military programs in disguise; and on and on.

-- Finally, this collapse of support solidified a certain kind of cognitive infrastructure within NASA -- the trench mentality. The agency as a whole has spent a lot of time acting as if it felt powerless and insecure. This can be seen in any number of ways: the agency's reluctance to even talk about any great vision; its willingness to do anything to protect existing programs and the viability of the centers, up to and including putting all the eggs in one basket -- the Shuttle; and its perversion of the "can do" attitude into a near total inability to say "Hey, wait a minute!" Whatever may have been done or said by individuals, the system as a whole somehow found it very difficult to step back and say "No, we can't develop the Shuttle on a budget that keeps getting arbitrarily cut from year to year," or "No, we can't make the Shuttle 'cost-effective' by political fiat," or "No, we can't keep cutting corners to meet a politically imposed launch rate."

This leads to a second truism about infrastructures:

TRUISM #2: INFRASTRUCTURES TAKE ON A LIFE OF THEIR OWN; OR, TO A MAN WITH A HAMMER, EVERYTHING LOOKS LIKE A NAIL

Whenever a commitment to a major piece of infrastructure is made, whether it's a highway like the Capital Beltway or Boston's Route 128, or a Space Shuttle, or even an institution such as NASA, it soon becomes apparent that the commitment is much more than concrete, hardware, and organization charts. Money is spent, investments are made, other alternatives are abandoned, new opportunities open up, people make career decisions, new businesses, new communities, and new bureaucracies spring up -- all utterly dependent on this infrastructure. Over time, thousands or even millions of people come to have a stake in things as they are. And the infrastructure itself, be it hardware or firmware, becomes like a part of the fabric of the universe. In fact, there's a marvelous process of feedback at work: it starts with conceptions of what the Nation can do, these conceptions are crystallized into tools -- infrastructure -- that help realize our conceptions, and then the infrastructure in turn begins to shape and color what the Nation can conceive of doing in the future.

The 1970s and early 1980s -- the Shuttle era before Challenger -- is an illustration of this. In one sense, of course, this era contradicts everything previously mentioned. It wasn't an era of continuity at all. Quite the opposite: not only was NASA trying to reinvent its whole space transportation infrastructure by replacing ELV's with the Shuttle, but the space community as a whole -- and eventually even the country as a whole -- was experiencing a change in the perception of space. Without ever explicitly deciding to, perceptions shifted from thinking of space as a frontier to thinking of space as resource -- a place to do useful things. This led in turn to a new perception of what the space program ought to be: instead of trying to win some kind of "space race," the U.S. should be pursuing the cost-effective exploitation of space.

Here, however, the exception proves the rule. One big reason for the change in perception was that the very existence of the Shuttle led people to start thinking seriously about what they could do with regular access to space. In other words, a new piece of infrastructure helped foster a new conception of what was possible and what was desirable. Another reason was that, starting in the 1960s and continuing even more strongly in the 1970s, the (mostly unmanned) U.S. space program provided what amounted to a proof of principle that there were useful or desireable things to be done up there: Communications, military reconnaissance, weather and land remote sensing, space astronomy, solar system exploration. Not only did the U.S. demonstrate that the technology was mature and that space was ready for exploitation, but an experienced cadre of scientists, spacecraft designers, rocket engineers, and the like -- a kind of human infrastructure -- was also built, all of whom had a stake in exploiting space, and all of whom were ready to take the next step.

This exception also proves the rule because of the way NASA went about preparing for the new era. The agency persuaded itself and the country that the way to achieve a "cost effective" space program was to put everything into a small fleet of reusable, all-purpose vehicles -- the shuttles. Furthermore, those vehicles were going to be state-of-the-art workhorses designed, developed, operated, and funded by the government. In other words, the mental model that took hold in the Sputnik/Apollo era was still dominant: space was still a big, expensive, heroic undertaking, and it was most emphatically still NASA's turf. NASA was not necessarily wrong to do things this way, it was simply very hard for anyone to conceive of doing things differently. Serious questioning of the government monopoly of the space program began only in the early 1980s, when agitation about private sector launch services emerged. Interestingly enough, that agitation was coming from exactly the same cadre of rocket engineers and spacecraft designers that had begun to perceive that they had a stake in demonstrating that NASA no longer had a monopoly on expertise.

And this leads to the third and final truism about infrastructures:

TRUISM #3: INFRASTRUCTURES DO CHANGE

As the foregoing suggests, infrastructures undergo continual metamorphosis under the pressure of time and events. The space program clearly went through some radical changes during the 1970s, from hardware to cognitive software. And the program is clearly going through some radical changes now, in the wake of the Challenger accident, though it may be too early to say just what those changes are going to be. To quote an anonymous source: "It's hard to predict -- especially the future." What we can do, however, is learn from the past. In the area of infrastructure, some fundamental questions can help in clarifying what options may be available in the future.

First, a simple question: what was wrong with the pre-Challenger space program?

A special report in *Business Week* called "The Productivity
Paradox" offers a useful analogy. The article asks why U.S.
manufacturers have spent roughly $17 billion on factory
automation during the past decade with so little to show for it.
The answer: managers typically base their decisions about what
kind of equipment to buy on the basis of standard accounting
methods, in which the payoff from automation is considered to
be equal to the savings in labor costs. That's it. As the editors
of *Business Week* pointed out, however, that equality ignores
certain payoffs from automation that are often much more
important -- the ability to operate with smaller inventories of raw
materials, for example; better quality control (and fewer defective
products); a streamlined assembly line through the use of
CAD/CAM to design parts with better "manufacturability;" and
increased flexibility to adapt to new product lines. All of these
are factors that are difficult for accountants to quantify. Yet they
all contribute heavily to the bottom line. *Business Week*'s point
was that, when these factors are taken into account, they often
lead managers to make a very different set of decisions about
what kind of automation to buy.

The analogy is obvious: how could the United States have
spent $XX billion dollars on the space program over the past two
decades and still have so little to show for it? If the question is
the same, then maybe the answer is the same: maybe the way
costs and benefits are defined, and the way decisions are made
about them -- our accounting system, metaphorically speaking --
has been leading us to answer the wrong questions. For example:

-- Prior to Challenger, official Washington accepted the idea
that a "cost effective" space program meant, in part,
achieving the "lowest price per pound to orbit." This was
partially because no one knew what it meant to be
"effective" when most of the benefits of space -- prestige,
etc. -- were so hard to quantify. The
lowest-price-per-pound measure, however, left out a
number of other factors, such as customer convenience,
schedule reliability, and the robustness of the Nation's
launch capability in the face of accidents and delay. The
result was a policy of reliance on the Shuttle and
unrealistic demands to get the Shuttle launch-rate up --
both leading ultimately to Challenger.

-- For budget managers at the OMB and in Congress,
another key question is whether or not an agency can keep

its budget level (or decreasing) from year to year. Programs all too often get stretched out to fit within an arbitrary funding envelope, thus costing far more than they would have otherwise. Multi-year budgeting would help, but it's certainly not a cure-all.

The level-budget syndrome shows up in other ways. Why, for example, does NASA always seem to be obsessed with hardware, as opposed to goals? Because hopes and aspirations don't appear as line items in the budget. Hardware does. Programs do. Institutions do. And since agency managers first have to sell these line items, and then devote virtually all their mental energy to defending them, the hardware very quickly becomes the goal. For much the same reason -- the agency's constant need to maintain a sales pitch -- there is the inevitable temptation to indulge in promises, hype, and "happytalk." Remember NASA's launch-rate lunacy prior to Challenger, and its inability to say "wait a minute" back in the 1970s? Remember NASA administrator Fletcher's "$200 per pound" promise back when he was trying to sell the Shuttle in 1972? Remember how NASA was going to take "the logical next step in space" and build a Space Station for only $8 billion? The fact is that the governmental system is not set up to encourage honesty: there's nothing to be gained from owning up to bad news if it can be avoided, and everything to be gained from assuring the powers that be that the program at hand is the biggest, the best, and absolutely essential to the national welfare.

Nothing mentioned here has changed since Challenger. The post-Challenger conventional wisdom suggests that the U.S. must have a mixed fleet and redundancy in launch systems. But by definition, redundancy means that you have more capacity than you "need." As such, redundancy may get slowly and steadily whittled away under pressure of the budget.

-- Another popular figure of merit in Washington is the famous "bringing-home-the-bacon" factor which, in the case of the space program, is often coupled with the "dazzle-me" factor. Thus, it's relatively easy to sell Congress on high-profile programs like the Shuttle or the Space Station: the presence of a human crew provides an inherent drama, and the cost can be mentally written off against the "national leadership" and "technological competitiveness" accounts. Unfortunately, however, this is not quite the same thing as supporting the broad-scale development of space. For example, most of the things that can be done in space -- earth remote sensing, space astronomy, weather forecasting, planetary exploration, etc. -- tend to be public goods. They benefit everybody. But the benefits are diffuse and hard to pinpoint. They rarely have the drama of a manned flight, and they rarely have well-heeled constituents with fire in their belly and a big stake in success. So even when Congress is supportive, as it often is, the system doesn't seem to feel much urgency about doing one of these public sector projects this year as opposed to next year or the year after. Worse, the system seems to feel even less urgency when it comes to things like scientific analysis, maintenance, and long term operations money. It's not hard to imagine why: when a Space Station or a space telescope is launched, it's an event, i.e. you know when you're done. The ribbon can be cut, so to speak. You can go on to something new. But operations and scientific analysis and maintenance are open-ended. They're never done. The money just keeps going out forever. And besides, it's boring, just like buying ammunition for the army. This could lead to further problems as operations money becomes very, very tight for the indefinite future.

In short, it has become painfully obvious in the three and one-half years since Challenger that the currently established mindsets -- whether in NASA, in Washington as a whole, or in the aerospace industry -- are not very well suited to any kind of rational exploitation of space. So the question becomes, How can these mindsets be changed?

Though difficult, it need not be impossible. Two conditions are necessary.

First, there has to be a shock to the system, a shock severe enough to convince people that the old order is no longer viable. The U.S. has certainly had a shock -- Challenger -- and it has certainly set the conventional wisdom reeling. It remains to be seen whether a change in administrations, coupled with the inevitable budget crunch, will finish the job.

Second, there has to be a clear and well-articulated alternative: not just a cry of rage at the way things are, but a new vision of what could be. Nobody is going to jump into the dark unless they have a place to jump *to*. In that context, it is significant that the conventional wisdom of the space program is being challenged by at least three new paradigms, which together may add up to precisely the kind of coherent alternative needed.

126

One, of course, is the idea of "private-sector infrastructure" -- the Conestoga rocket, private launch sites in Hawaii or Australia, the Industrial Space Facility, and so forth. This paradigm retains the space program's exploitation goal while cutting back the traditional government-monopoly role.

Private-sector space activities could be very beneficial. First, private-sector activity could give a lot of new people a very personal stake in space exploration (as opposed to feeding at the government trough). In an odd, psychological way, this may feed back and increase the legitimacy of government activities in space. It could reaffirm that government research investments in space really can pay off. Second, the customer orientation and simple-is-beautiful approach, which probably would characterize private-sector activities, could serve as a healthy antidote to NASA's "No-Bucks-Without-Buck-Rogers" obsession. Orbital Sciences Corporation claims that their new Pegasus rocket can accelerate approximately 100 kilograms or so to escape velocity for $5 or $10 million. Does anybody have a sensor or two they want to send to Mars *next year?!* And third, if a lot of infrastructure is built to support commercial activity in space it suddenly becomes much easier to do science and exploration as well. A Mars expedition, for example, could use existing commercial facilities at marginal cost instead of having to build them from scratch.

The second new paradigm is this idea of making space science and applications an equal partner to the manned space program, perhaps even in a new organization independent of NASA. In particular, as Riccardo Giacconi has suggested, the mission planners should have the authority to plan their own missions and to "buy" their own launch services from whomever they want, so that they can use their dollars most effectively. This idea clearly grows out of the scientists' immense frustration over being forced to use the Shuttle whether they needed the manned capability or not, and may have a lot of merit. Neither space science nor space applications have ever had any problem with "goals," so there would be little risk of this new organization floundering around. Furthermore, a strong emphasis on unmanned space operations would produce exactly the kind of research likely to have the most productive spinoffs back here on Earth: namely, robotics and automation.

Finally, there is the third new paradigm: the idea of a joint, U.S.--Soviet manned mission to Mars. Such a program could give the country (and Washington) a clear sense of what the manned space program is about, for the first time since Apollo, as well as give NASA a clear rationale for a space station and all the other hardware it wants to build. In short, it would validate an urge that's been hidden in the closet too long. Space isn't just about cold-war chauvinism and capitalism on the high frontier. As the National Commission on Space pointed out, it's about exploration, the expansion of the human race into the solar system.

This is one of the reasons for being enthusiastic about collaborating with the Soviets. Their technology may not be the greatest, and there's still a lot of reason for both sides to be suspicious. But one thing the Soviets do have is that sense of wonder, a sense of the infinite possibilities of space. Top-level Soviet space scientists talk about the colonization of the planets and the destiny of humankind with a zest that is straight out of 1950s science fiction. Americans haven't talked like that, at least officially, for twenty years. Maybe we have something to learn from them.

PART THREE

Bringing in Economics

A common theme running through many of these chapters is a concern that the civilian space program has been unduly preoccupied with large-scale engineering and development projects that have technical achievement as their only criterion for success. The next two chapters provide alternative approaches for injection of economic criteria into programs in order to provide management with broader, more utilitarian ways of measuring success.

Molly Macauley, an economist with Resources for the Future, points out a number of areas where the tools of the economist might be applied to assure more effective resource allocation. These include, not surprisingly, pricing policy for the Space Shuttle; policies for allocating resources -- e.g. power and crew time -- on the Space Station; deciding when to compete and when to cooperate in the international space arena; and the choice of manned or unmanned mission modes for space science projects. Macauley believes that, among key players in space policy, an understanding of "the role of economics remains primitive". She suggests some reasons why this may be true, but her major message is that times have changed, resources are scarce, hard choices must be made, and economics can help.

Jeffrey Struthers was deeply involved in the development of commercialization policies during his many years at the Office of Management and Budget. He believes that the commercialization of space will require closer government/industry relationships. There is a "clear difference between the situation with space and that for technologies having less strategic national importance and a less pervasive government presence. The traditional ideological concerns about the separation of government and industry will require some modification if commercial involvement is to grow in the U.S.".

Taking the two chapters together, Macauley shows how economics can improve programs and Struthers shows that in order to put economic forces to work we will have to involve industry in a new way.

Chapter 8

RETHINKING SPACE POLICY: THE NEED TO UNEARTH THE ECONOMICS OF SPACE

Molly K. Macauley[1]

Reprinted with permission from the William and Mary Review, *The Review*.

INTRODUCTION

The Nation's approach to space policy consistently misses the mark. The failure of policy, not technology or limits on the size of the NASA budget, in large part explains a slow down in space science, the lack of strategy for international cooperation and competition, faltering steps towards a Space Station, and the dislocations of the Challenger accident.

Many of the shortcomings of policy lie in poor economics. The most recent national space policy, announced in early 1988, is a case in point. That policy continued a longstanding failure to resolve a host of resource allocation issues *not only in commercial but in intragovernmental settings as well.* A notable example, graphically demonstrated by the roller coaster history of the Galileo program, is the pressing need for workable mechanisms, rather than the moral suasion advanced in the policy, for choosing between the shuttle and unmanned vehicles to launch space science payloads. This example, and numerous others, demonstrate how the lack of attention to effective resource allocation -- as distinguished from the issue of setting the budget itself -- causes the Nation's space program to operate well below its technological and economic potential. Worse, decisionmakers fail to realize that good economics ultimately redounds to their benefit, in freeing up additional resources for space activities without necessarily requiring increases in the federal space budget.

The paper proceeds as follows. The section below reviews the 1988 presidential space policy directive to point out two areas where improved economic thinking is crucial. These are access to space infrastructure, including next-generation space activities, and approaches to international cooperation and competition. The next two sections consider each of these areas, emphasizing where the role of economic analysis is most salient. A concluding section takes stock, ponders why the space program is primitive in making use of economics, and urges a new approach.

THE FLAWED ECONOMICS OF CURRENT SPACE POLICY

The 1988 space policy has four themes. It seeks to clarify the respective responsibilities of various federal agencies, advance the role of the private sector, foster international cooperation and competition, and reaffirm support for major public investments in space. Specifically, the policy:

-- Emphasizes a "separation of powers" for the oversight and conduct of space activities by government agencies. Jurisdictional responsibility is divided among NASA and the Departments of Commerce, Transportation, State, and Defense. The policy also continues the role of an existing interagency group on space involving these agencies as well as the Office of Management and Budget, the Office of

Science and Technology Policy, and additional defense-related offices.[2]
-- Advocates a larger and more direct role for the private sector in space. The policy endorses specific private sector proposals, including a commercially owned and operated space station, the refurbishment of the Space Shuttle's external fuel tanks as space laboratories, and a module to increase the living and working area on the Space Shuttle. It also outlines guidelines for federal procurement of commercial space transportation services and the private sector use of federal launch facilities.
-- Urges international competition as well as cooperation in space.
-- Calls for public investment in space transportation, commercial and NASA Space Stations, and certain technologies, collectively labeled the "Pathfinder" program, deemed necessary for future manned space exploration.

At first glance, these themes appear timely and comprehensive. Yet the rocky course of the policy in subsequent Congressional deliberations calls into question its effectiveness. In fact, a closer review of the policy suggests shortcomings that center on the failure to address fundamentally economic issues:

It is far from clear that the policy has smoothed the conduct of space decisionmaking, most notably where economic problems loom at the intersection of responsibility among federal offices. The approaches of government departments remain antagonistically disparate in these areas despite the effort to balance interagency roles. For instance, within weeks after the policy was announced strong disagreement arose between the Departments of Transportation and Commerce, the OMB, and others, on one side, and NASA, on the other, over pricing Space Shuttle transportation -- a central element of space activity. That argument is likely to resurface now that the shuttle is again operating; caught in-between will be commercial as well as government interests in access to space.

The new policy also fails to accommodate the Congressional setting. A particularly adversarial relationship between Congress and the executive branch has followed in the wake of the policy, with argument focusing on shuttle pricing and the Space Station. As long as government remains central to space activity -- and, private sector initiatives notwithstanding, the new directive perpetuates this role -- the Congress is the ultimate decisionmaker by way of budget authority. This is the situation not only when appropriations are directly made for projects such as the Space Station, but also when legislation affects key aspects of space, as it does in having codified shuttle pricing.

True business autonomy remains elusive. To be sure, the policy outlines relationships between government and industry in two important areas of space transportation: procurement and regulation. In the case of these and other commercial space activities advocated by the policy, however, the distinction between private and government remains almost indistinguishable. Government continues to be involved at almost all junctures in the course of doing business, retaining major roles as predominant customer (for example, it could lease 70% of the commercial station), regulator, gatekeeper at the launchpad and at the borders of international trade, and importantly, banker.

The policy calls for both international cooperation and competition but fails to provide guidelines for which, when, and with whom. In fact, the National Security Council's Director for Space Policy was asked the following while fielding questions about the new directive: The policy urges the government to purchase commercial launch services whenever commercial launch services will do the job. Is it possible, then, that the U.S. government would purchase a launch from the European company, Arianespace? The answer was merely that the question had not come up.

Another area where decisions of international scope need to be made, but where the new policy offers little guidance, is in funding space for the purpose of U.S. leadership -- a frequent refrain in the policy. It variously states that leadership requires U.S. preeminence or eminence in specific areas of space activity, yet it fails to identify these areas. Rather, the usual set of policy goals is listed: ensuring national security, enhancing international prestige, and obtaining scientific, technical, and economic gain. The problem is that not all of these goals are jointly served by the same set of space activities, and the policy definitely shirks making the hard choices that are required in a climate of fiscal restraint.

The policy fails to provide a framework for evaluating key public investment. Major funding decisions, rather than being well-marshalled by the policy as they proceeded through Congressional budget deliberations, were stymied in the course of those negotiations. Debate over a Space Station is the most notable example. The new policy had as its centerpiece both a commercial and a NASA station, but throughout debate the purposes of each were left unclear, as was the extent to which the stations would be complementary or substitutable in attaining those aims. Also unaddressed systematically or objectively were other obvious but crucial questions: What would be the full cost of either approach? What would be the benefit? Where is evidence of willingness to pay by federal users, purported to include agencies other than NASA? One rationale implied by the new policy in supporting the commercial Space Station is that contracting-out by government for goods and services has been cost effective in other federal activities. Is that argument fully supportable in the case of the commercial station? If so, how is it consistent with the new policy's simultaneous support of the NASA station?

Answers to these questions would not have been without controversy, nor would they have been deterministic in deciding the fate of either station. Posing them would, however, have led to significantly more informed public debate. It would also have conformed to the analysis required (by executive order) of practically every other major public investment.[3] And it would have obviated the delay that is likely to be imposed by the actual Congressional outcome, including remanding the issue for analysis of these very questions.

These essentially economic problems in part reflect issues that are directly related to a space program built on infrastructure, not a one-shot Apollo program. They also relate to the interface of federal and private space activity, and to the increasing scope of space activity in other countries. That these problems persist in the wake of the new directive suggests the need to rethink approaches to space policy. In particular, what might be called "policy" infrastructure, constituting improved institutional and financial management of "technology" infrastructure, is now required in key areas of economic import if the directive's ambition to set U.S. space activities on course is to make headway.

ACCESS TO SPACE INFRASTRUCTURE: SHUTTLE AND SPACE STATION PRICING POLICY

One area for improvement is shuttle pricing. A rational and long-term policy is fundamental to the conduct of space activity. But such pricing has yet to be implemented, despite a shuttle program that, dating from concept studies when pricing policy should have been set forth, is over a decade old.

The present policy maintains a price well below true resource cost, and also proscriptively rations access to payloads arbitrarily deemed "shuttle unique." Once the shuttle system is operating regularly again, below-cost pricing will perpetuate the shuttle-dependence that has already brought adverse consequences to space science and to the conventional rocket industry. Moreover, the vague criterion of shuttle uniqueness could assume vast import and attract correspondingly lengthy arbitration.

Proscriptive rationing thus does not eliminate the need for pricing policy; rather, economically correct pricing would eliminate the need for such a criterion. Furthermore, estimates of shuttle fees that more fairly reflect the true resource cost suggest that the shuttle and unmanned launchers remain cost-competitive at some payload capacities -- in other words, shuttle proponents need not fear that a consequence of improved shuttle fees would necessarily be damaging to the program. On the contrary, improved pricing would probably enhance the program.[4]

A second area is Space Station pricing. Here, a decade of problematic shuttle pricing history with its ill side effects is about to repeat itself, and be magnified to encompass not only the space transportation system but a Space Station as well. Effective allocation of scarce station resources, such as electricity, water, communications, laboratory space, and crew time, will go far in helping to realize the station's scientific, technological, and economic potential -- or in demonstrating that the station is a bad idea.

In addition, greater attention to these issues during past years would have led to more informed discussion over the decision to build the station. Yet, as the National Research Council pointed out in reviewing station costs, NASA's approach to cost estimation is fundamentally flawed, even in straightforward enumeration of resources required to build a station (for example, shuttle flights for station construction were omitted from NASA calculations).[5] Neither a commercial station leased by government nor a government station can avoid such issues of resource allocation. In the recent debate over both facilities, for example, the issue is prominently reflected by the need to ascertain whether it is worth it for the government to commit $700 million to lease a commercial facility. The homework has not been done to bring adequate information to bear in answering this question.

Also lost in the debate focusing on subsidizing the transport of a commercial station has been this fact: No matter how much a commercial station operator pays for transportation, the rest of the bill will be paid. There is no free launch. What is fundamental to the debate over the commercial station, as well as subsidies to users to cover operating costs of a NASA station, is that the size of the subsidies, and their long-term implications, be explicitly measured and made part of the decision process. At issue is defining a standard that forces the implications of pricing decisions related to one space activity to be evaluated with a view to their consequences for other space activities.

To be avoided, then, is the danger that ineffective pricing decisions in one area of space activity introduce ineffectiveness in another. In this regard, it should be noted that the recent space directive prohibits "direct subsidies" to commercial space activity. "Direct" is not defined (are subsidies for shuttle transport of a commercial station direct or indirect?), nor are guidelines given on what constitute economic costs, critical benchmarks for recognizing a subsidy. It is hidden subsidies, arising either "indirectly" or simply ignored in public debate, that can distort decisions and ultimately undermine public policy. The most obvious examples are the standstill in business for unmanned launchers caused by underpricing the shuttle during the early 1980s, and the upward bias in estimates of shuttle demand -- again, biases resulting from several years of below-cost pricing -- that may well have overstated the need to replace Challenger.

Pricing decisions also need to be viewed with respect to their implications for the longer term, as that is the timeframe that now is relevant to space planning. As an example, Congress has mandated that the station make full use of automated technologies as they become available. Despite the mandate, the useful substitution of artificial intelligence for human involvement may well be bypassed if the costs of labor or crew time are hidden. A similar argument has of course been made by proponents of unmanned space activity, and reappears again in debate over next generation launch technology. Seldom acknowledged in the argument, however, is the powerful role effective pricing could play in signalling relative costs of automation versus human involvement. That difference unfortunately eludes public debate over manned activities undertaken for national prestige; worse, however, is when it is not part of decisions over those activities we want to become routine.[6]

STRATEGIES FOR THE INTERNATIONAL ARENA: WHEN TO COOPERATE AND WHEN TO COMPETE

The recent policy sets forth a challenging goal in arguing for international leadership in *all* areas of space, because if it is not already, it will soon be too expensive to be dominant in all activities -- launches, communications, life sciences, materials processing, remote sensing. Moreover, even if it were possible, it may not even be desirable to be preeminent in all areas, as

138

activities differ markedly in terms of how much they benefit
national security, international prestige, or scientific and economic
gain.

As more nations become technologically capable of competing
with the U.S. than in the past, the spoils may accrue most to the
victor who recognizes and exploits opportunities for growing
interdependence in certain activities, thereby freeing resources to
pursue preeminence in other areas. Devising such a strategy
indeed involves hard choices. The problem to date is that the
argument of fostering international leadership is submitted by all
special interests in the space community, and no one has
scrutinized the relative merits of various programs.

Yet such choices can be made effectively. The effort could in
part draw substantial guidance from a growing body of research
in contemporary economics, political science, and history of
science that focuses on "second mover" advantages in technology
development and management. For instance, one blueprint for
choice could come from analysis of benefits to the U.S. in
following the lead of other nations in aircraft and jet
manufacturing. In cases where benefits are intangible,
representing national prestige or the augmentation of scientific
knowledge, the analysis could draw from increasingly adept -- and
politically accepted -- economic methodologies for valuing public
goods.

To be sure, arguing to delay any aspect of space technology
development may be perceived as an heretical argument for a
second- best position and thus politically untenable. But
ineffective pursuit of leadership may ultimately be damaging --
politically, economically, and technologically. Researchers in
space science now cite such harm as the legacy of short-sighted
decisions about shuttle policy. This experience will continue as
the rule rather than the exception unless a selective approach to
developing new technologies can be both rationally designed and
made politically feasible.

In addition to the problem of investing for U.S. leadership,
issues also loom concerning the competitive position of U.S. space
industries. For instance, decisions are being made regarding the
extent of federal assistance by way of insurance limits or other
subsidies to the commercial launch industry. Here, the terms of
assistance need careful consideration for two reasons. First, a
large fraction of projected customers are foreign, in which case
subsidies to insurance benefit foreign consumers. The launch
industry notes, however, that protecting the industry secures a
national launch capability, and jobs. Both arguments need more

rigorous consideration than they have been given to date, particularly as they have different implications for the size and nature of government protection. Speaking speculatively, such review may find that any case for industry protection must rest on national security concerns rather than the preservation of employment. This is because, based on industry employment projections, only about 8000 U.S. jobs are involved.

Two additional observations on the international posture of the U.S. involve the increasing focus of other countries on their own autonomy in space, and the implications for the U.S. of the spending patterns of other countries. The new policy presumes that taking the initiative in selecting areas in which to compete or to cooperate is to be the prerogative of the United States. That may not be fully practicable now, nor likely to be so in the future. The past ten years have brought an increasing frequency of public statements in which other countries cite the attainment and preservation of national autonomy as a driver in their space programs.[7] What U.S. strategies for international action best comport with foreign autonomy? One strategy is the design not only of so-called clean technical interfaces in joint missions but clean economic interfaces, attainable with effective pricing and other financial guidelines. Progress to date on international participation in the Space Station has been halting in large part for this very reason. Memoranda of Understanding as have now been signed are not particularly reassuring, as their mix of cost-sharing and barter-like arrangements will attract perennial Congressional and foreign government tinkering.

Also on the subject of international cooperation and competition, it is not obvious what to infer from the fact that the U.S. spends about $30 per person, not counting activities financed by private industry, and Europe spends about $3 per person on space; maybe the U.S. gets less for its money? Certainly that is an argument surfacing in cross-country comparisons of spending on education and health care, where the assumption that more spending is better has not been substantiated.

It is significant that the rate of spending on space activity by Europe and Japan has increased markedly in recent years relative to their gross national product, meaning that the share of national resources allocated to space activity is increasing. This is the case even though these countries are well below the U.S. in terms of purchasing power parity, a measure of wealth that tries to account for differences in the cost of living. On this marketbasket basis of wealth, the average Japanese is still about 30 percent poorer than the average American, and the average person in France, Italy and

140

Britain a little worse off than that. This in large part explains the perennial debate in Britain, the fourth largest ESA contributor, concerning the size of its ESA contribution, and foretells increasing argument, not unlike our budgetary deliberations, over increases in space expenditure by other countries.

Consequently, arguments about who's spending and how much need greater analysis in the case of space before they can credibly support either alarm or complacency about the effectiveness and comparative position of the U.S. space program. Only then can an assessment be made of the plethora of articles like the following, each with a different country filling in the blank: "Is _____ Losing the Technological Race?" Public discussion in the U.S. presumes that it is "the United States," but recently, in an article by two British scholars, the blank read "Western Europe."[8] Even a prominent Soviet cosmonaut has claimed that the Soviet space program suffers from a lack of purposefulness and consistency, is unsystematic, and has no precise formulation of goals and how to achieve them stage by stage. Again, only the name of the country has been changed in lodging this typically American complaint.[9]

THE NEED FOR ECONOMIC ANALYSIS

As nations thus continue to play each other off in budget matching, racing to develop technology, and so on, it will become even clearer that space activities undertaken for national prestige and technological leadership come at an increasingly high price. Unless these costs are measured, understood, and used in decisionmaking, the pursuit of other objectives -- domestic economic gain, scientific advance -- are in turn distorted. For instance, a decision to subsidize the shuttle or the domestic U.S. launch industry to keep launch prices below the price of foreign launchers imposes tangible costs, regardless of whether foreign launchers are subsidized as well. Likewise, a decision to focus on manned activity also involves calculable costs that may be several times higher than alternative unmanned technologies. In these or other decisions, there is nothing wrong with paying these costs, provided that public debate is sufficiently informed to make these tradeoffs wisely, and anticipate their secondary consequences (in the second example, delayed development of automation and a slow down in space science, and in the first example, subsequent rounds of price retaliation by foreign launchers).

Yet an understanding among key players of the role of economics remains primitive. There appear to be three reasons:

First, space is expensive and we would rather just not know that.

Second, a twenty-year-old mindset lingers, that of the abundantly funded Apollo project.

Third, there is a befuddlement -- professed or sincere -- about how a price tag can be put on space activities, particularly as they are undertaken as a matter of national pride, well being, prestige, and sheer thrill.

The fallacies are, of course, these:

It is in fact because space is expensive -- its budget is a large target for social welfare -- that economic analysis and cogent argument matter in managing the space program. The fiscal importance of being unimportant is not an option for space (at least not yet).

Concerning the Apollo mindset: in marked contrast to that program, which was richly funded and had a single goal, scarce fiscal means pursue competing ends today. The force is not with us -- the force being the ability to marshall focused public support in a post-Sputnik decade. Today, whether rightly or wrongly, many Americans shrug off the Soviet space station if they are aware of it at all. Unless apathy is the result of an uninformed populace, it tends to indict the U.S. station as a worthwhile project; at the very least, such apathy weakens support for the station. Either situation -- that of decisionmakers who have faltered in public education and outreach, or a well-informed populace that is lukewarm towards a U.S. station -- calls for a change in tack compared with the approach to Apollo. Meanwhile, other activities -- fusion energy, medical research -- compete for headlines and the science budget.

Can price tags be put on space? Well, they are necessarily placed on other things fundamental to well-being -- such as decisions about how many food stamps a family of four receives. We put them on our own activities in willingness to pay for a designer car or other prestigious items. There are two rules here: decisions always imply values for the outputs and interests served by them; and decisions are often better made if fully informed.

For example, recall the concern over quality of the environment in the 1960s. For centuries society had been free to pollute, and it polluted freely. In revolt, the 1960s brought demands for clean air and water at any cost. More recently this theme has been confronted in the handling of hazardous waste. Clean air and water, the siting of wastes, and mitigating the risks of exposure and premature death from toxic chemicals are if not more so, then certainly as emotive and hard to value in public debate as is space.

But in the case of the environment, more quantitative and rigorous evaluation of its economics, and the making of hard choices, culminated in the successful use of price-based mechanisms for pollution control. A result has been environmental quality conforming to standards, in many cases at lower cost than traditional, purely technological control measures. Incidentally, these price-based mechanisms were instituted not during a Republican administration, but by the Carter administration. Moreover, techniques for explicit public valuation studies of clean water have actually been codified by the Environmental Protection Agency and Army Corps of Engineers, and such approaches are now being used by researchers considering how and where to site hazardous waste facilities. Finally, as noted earlier, cost-benefit review is routinely required for environmental regulation, as well as all federal regulatory policy and associated major public projects.

The point of this lengthy example is that handling the environment involved significant value-laden and emotional debate, and large public expenditures. Yet the Nation is sorting these out. In like fashion, it can also be done for space.

There is one additional point to make concerning the salience of this example. Public valuation studies of environmental quality have found that society tends to place a greater value on, and is willing to pay more for, the aesthetic and amenity benefits of clean air and water -- recreation, a blue sky -- than direct health benefits. Such a finding in turn provides guidance for allocating environmental expenditures. In the case of space, it may be that public preferences favor spending on Pathfinder leading to Solar System exploration, for instance, over spending to obtain near-term, direct economic benefits from space activity. Such a result would, by way of improving understanding of public constituency, assist Congress and others in making hard budgetary decisions.

To sum up, space policy needs policy infrastructure: pricing policy, explicit realization of opportunity costs of various space activities, and Congressional and executive decisions made on the basis of informed public understanding. In contrast to the old attitudes -- those formed by the well-funded but single goal of Apollo -- today, scarce fiscal means and numerous areas of scientific endeavor other than space activities pursue competing ends -- leadership, prestige, commercial gain. Deciding how to use the means, what science to do, is not primarily a technological problem. As much creativity and vision as has been devoted to space technologies, and as much effort as was given to developing the recent policy pronouncement, necessarily now needs to be brought to bear on steps to implement that pronouncement.

NOTES

1. Responsibility for opinions in this chapter rests with the author alone. Appreciation is extended to *The Review* of the College of William and Mary for the illustration.

2. The recently proposed National Space Council may focus on space and technology interests, but it is not obvious that management or budgetary concerns would be fully ameliorated.

3. See Executive Order 12291 (*Federal Register* 46 (19 February 1981): 13193-98.)

4. The shuttle pricing debate has traditionally misused terminology, as well, with "true resource cost" often erroneously taken to mean "full cost recovery." True resource cost in fact falls in between full cost pricing recovery and so-called "additive cost" pricing; their definitions are outside the scope of the paper, but what is germane to the argument above is that a more correct understanding of true resource cost during the policy debate would probably please all parties, both those advocating the recouping of full costs as well as those arguing to recoup out-of-pocket expenses. For a fuller discussion of shuttle pricing, see Toman, M. and M. Macauley, "No Free Launch: Efficient Space Transportation Pricing," *Land Economics* Vol. 65, no. 2 (May 1989), p. 1-9.

5. See National Research Council, "Report of the Committee on the Space Station" (National Academy Press, September 1987). This point corroborates the observation about poor economic literacy in the space program -- see the previous note.

6. For further discussion of the long-term implications of resource allocation on a space station, see Macauley, M., "Decision Time for Allocating Resources on the Space Station" *Resources*, Vol. 89 (Fall 1987), pp. 5-7.

7. For example, see D. Dickson, "Europe Moves Toward 'Full Autonomy' in Space" *Europe* 47 (December 1987), pp. 26-27.

8. See P. Patel and K. Pavitt, "Is Western Europe Losing the Technological Race?" *Research Policy* Vol. 16 (August 1987), pp. 59-85.

9. See "Cosmonaut Faults Soviet Space Program" *Science* Vol. 239, no. 4836 (8 January 1988), p. 140.

Chapter 9

ENCOURAGING A U.S. COMMERCIAL SPACE INDUSTRY

Jeffrey Struthers

THE HIGHEST AND BEST FORM OF EFFICIENCY IS THE
SPONTANEOUS COOPERATION OF A FREE PEOPLE.

WOODROW WILSON

Space activities fall largely in three categories. There are
activities resulting from *public investments in support of public
objectives* (e.g., defense, exploration, weather forecasting, scientific
research), activities resulting from *private investment in support of
private objectives* (e.g., numerous communications satellites); and
activities resulting from *private investment in support of a mix of
public and private objectives* (e.g., commercial launch services,
commercial remote sensing).

Since 1984, the Reagan Administration has put public emphasis
on encouraging greater commercial use of space, i.e., activities
involving greater private investment in space technologies and the
use of space. This theme, which began with NASA initiatives in
1984, was given added emphasis in the Reagan space policy issued
earlier this year. However, the commercial uses of space on a
significant scale have been underway now for nearly thirty years.
Of course, the largest use by far has been for satellite-based
communications, but other smaller space industries have emerged
dealing with secondary products, such as space-derived data for
commercial weather forecasting and value-added remote sensing
services. More recently, commercial launch services have gotten

underway, and commercial navigation appears to be coming fast. Many also see the prospects for highly valuable diagnostic services and materials production in the microgravity environment. But in the U.S. the dominant user of space and investor in space remains, analogous to every other space-faring nation in the world, largely the U.S. government. And the only major, primarily commercial industry in space today remains that of communications satellites.

The barriers to accelerating greater commercial investment and involvement in space activities are reflected in the history of space activity and the differing motivations of the players. To those of us who would use space as a place to position satellites for practical uses, such as commercial research, analysis, and production, weather forecasting, and national security, we often hear the phrase "space is a place, not a mission." This catchphrase reflects the obvious concern that where practical or economic objectives are concerned, space-based activity must compete with ground-based alternatives. But "Space" is also a mission and a frontier. Exploration, the pursuit of knowledge of the universe, and man's involvement in space have been implicit national goals and the central missions of NASA since its founding in 1958.

Many of the founders of modern rocket technology were inspired by the potential of the technology for exploration of space frontiers. But the initial development of space technology occurred in pursuit of space as a medium for the efficient movement of weapons. In fact, the motive for this use of space was strongly in evidence well before the twentieth century, in the use of military rockets. And it was this technology, which was tremendously expanded in the interests of national security during and immediately following World War II, that provided the basis in 1957 for the beginnings of the U.S. national security and civil space programs.

In one important respect, this evolution is similar to that of aeronautics, where balloons demonstrated their utility for military applications before the twentieth century and powered aircraft became accepted weapons platforms during World War I. But in the case of powered flight in the atmosphere, commercial applications were more readily apparent, and crude but commercially useful applications of the technology were achievable by entrepreneurs from the earliest days of powered flight. Aeronautics, therefore, quickly became important to both the military and the economy, and aviation grew up in a mixed government/commercial environment.

By contrast, space, before Sputnik, grew largely into a military domain in every nation seeking its use. Hence, space became closely controlled and protected by government in every space-faring nation of the world. Technological achievements were often made under the cloak of secrecy. In the U.S., the systems used in space were produced largely by weapons producers who competed to produce highly sophisticated, specialized and high risk products for a single customer, the U.S. government. With the advent of the Apollo program, the motivations changed somewhat, but these primary characteristics of U.S. space activities remained largely unchanged. The space business enjoyed few of the characteristics that enabled the commercial development of the highly successful aeronautics industry with the help of NASA's predecessor, the National Advisory Committee for Aeronautics.

As a result, space technology and operations today reflect a predominant government culture. Although the U.S. government now has 30 years of experience with space technology, capabilities that have resulted in acceptable achievement of government missions are frequently difficult to transfer to commercial practice.

The technologies, often "big ticket" items designed for peak performance for specialized application, or to maintain high performance despite the conflicting needs of multiple users, are often not well matched to commercial needs.

Current developers and suppliers of equipment and services for the government space programs are often not commercially-oriented.

Key space technologies are interdependent, technically and economically. Thus, designing a cheap satellite may not be helpful if launch costs or costs of other government provided infrastructure prevent overall venture costs from being competitive.

Moreover, even where government-developed capabilities are suitable for initial commercial activities, government and commercial users must compete for limited capacity (e.g., ground processing, launch and flight operations).

Some restrictions will also be imposed by government upon commercial activities simply because of government's need to oversee the use and dissemination of technologies with military potential. These restrictions will inhibit the ability of firms in the international marketing of some space products and services.

Finally, it is clear that the space programs of other nations are likely to remain closely government-held and sponsored. The French Ariane and Spot programs enjoy the fruits of government-supported activities analogous to those in the U.S. Moreover, because other nations are standing on our shoulders as the technology matures, there are likely to be an increasing number of foreign government-backed competitors in this game. In this case, as with some international airlines, government-backed organizations, driven by political as well as profit motives, will be competing with U.S. private sector firms.

So, if it is so difficult, why encourage a commercial space industry at all? Why not just admit that this is an inherently government business and leave it at that?

First, the U.S. private sector has an awesome reputation for innovation and making markets grow, and may do so in space if given proper motivation to become involved, just as it did with aviation. One could expect lower costs and increased capacity for space goods and services. If development of a commercial space industry were to evolve like other successful industries, one could also expect new uses as capacity increases and costs go down, and as access to space and related support services become routine and reliable.

We also know of possibilities, not yet proven to be competitive with ground-based alternatives, such as process research in a gravity-free environment, and microgravity commercial activities such as the production of medicines, the conduct of diagnostics, or the production of catalysts in space. There are also potential commercial concepts emerging for communications including mobile communications, direct broadcast, and ties with cable systems; new uses for remote sensing for crop assessment and resource exploration; continued improvements in weather prediction and severe storm warning; and world-wide search and rescue and navigation systems. If feasible and not critically impeded by the other barriers mentioned, the economic potential of these concepts may be realized. Other nations are seeing this potential and are acting to help position their industries to take advantage of it. These opportunities are good examples of where private investments may be raised in pursuit of private purposes.

Lower costs and increased capacity are essential to fully tap the purely commercial potential of space, but they are also required for the government to meet its own goals. With the continuing fiscal crisis, this potential confluence of public and private goals is a major opportunity for the U.S. to achieve its goals more efficiently and more rapidly, but it has not yet been fully explored by either government or industry.

There is also confluence in other ways. The tenure of the U.S. civil space program is currently about that of Federal career civil servants. Young professionals who entered the government space program in the Apollo era are now retiring or approaching retirement in the senior scientific and management ranks of government. Government is soon to face a major drain in its pool of senior technical and managerial talent, which will be difficult to replace in the continuing environment of restraints in the Federal workforce. Thus, a greater reliance by government on commercially provided facilities and services in space will become an increasingly attractive alternative to government capital investment and management. Acceleration of commercial investment and management will allow government to focus on those aspects which it does best, such as space exploration and the support of basic scientific research and generic technology development and validation. Thus, there are also opportunities for large private investments to be raised in pursuit of a mix of public and private purposes.

Unfortunately, the synergy that is possible through the common pursuit of public and private purposes is being effectively blocked by the barriers noted earlier. It is true that many firms are investing in research in space, to investigate what is possible, and to stay abreast of the state of the art and emerging opportunities. However, the reality is that there can be no significant mass of additional private investment for purposes other than communications satellites until the barriers are reduced or removed. The reality is that, for the near term, certainly until the Space Station flies in the mid-1990s, the government will continue to represent the dominant share of the market outside of communications satellites.

What should be apparent from this is the clear difference between the situation with space and that for technologies having less strategic national importance and a less pervasive historical government presence. The traditional ideological concerns about separation of government and industry will require some modification if commercial involvement in space is to grow in the U.S. There is every reason to believe it will grow internationally. Space is not an arena in which government is intruding upon the heretofore sacred province of industry. Rather it is a case of encouraging inroads by industry into an area heretofore dominated by government, here and abroad. Nor is it fundamentally a matter of displacing performance by government, although this will probably occur eventually to some degree. Rather, the notion is to expand the market for U.S. produced space goods and services. This expansion should start with existing commercial and government markets but should be encouraged to continue in directions which will find industry in position to capture a growing share of a growing market.

One does not have to believe in a strong government role in

setting industrial policy to appreciate that government will always have a strong role in space ... because space is both a place and a mission, and space technologies are of strategic national importance. The U.S. space program must have substantial industrial and commercial components if the U.S. is to take advantage of its strengths and compete with other nations. And the space program must also involve universities working with other sectors because of the long-term character of many space activities and the need to assure an adequate flow of new skills as the industry evolves.

Similarly, space is an arena in which government regulation and control is so pervasive that there is no reasonable fear that a monopoly will emerge out of unbridled competition to gouge the consumer or the government. Indeed, it should not be frightening to the U.S taxpayer to have one of its industries achieve an outstanding world market share and contribute strongly towards the balance of trade. Given the pressing and continuing importance of the trade deficit, it is in the U.S. taxpayers' interest to recognize and support the inherent mixed-sector character of this business. We, as beneficiaries of this involvement, should encourage government to work in partnership with business to make the space market grow and to establish a leading market share for industry, and therefore, for the Nation's economy.

The scale of investment and scope of human talent and research facilities required to establish space infrastructure and compete with government-backed industries of other nations is large by any measure. These resources are not likely to be aggregated without some active encouragement by government. Thus, it is ironic that with the increasing demand for improving U.S. competitiveness, an emerging trend today in the aerospace industry is for U.S. companies to team with similar companies abroad, but to avoid teaming with other competent U.S. firms because of the chilling spectre of anti-trust. We are talking of the need to codify relaxation of anti-trust statutes, not by policy, but by law.

The key word here is partnership between government and industry, rather than competition or confrontation. Partnership is what makes the difference between success and failure in many businesses, and so it will be in space. Partnership means making a commitment to working together towards common goals, with each party accepting certain responsibilities towards the other. And partnership is what must be achieved between business and government to accelerate the transition to a stronger balance of U.S. commercial space activity. This is not to deny the necessary role of some regulation, such as the Department of Transportation role with respect to the commercial launch vehicle industry. Rather, it is to highlight the need to enable or allow initiatives involving both Government and industry.

With an appropriate and effective partnership between government and industry, it is reasonable to expect that private investment can, over the long term, parallel in space that which has made the U.S. a leader in aeronautics. For example, government can enable widespread private investment by helping to establish the ability to get to and from space reliably, economically, and routinely; by helping to demonstrate the ability to live and work in space; and by demonstrating that government and industry can perform as reliable partners in major, long-term space activities.

For such a partnership, Government and industry must:

-- Better define a national consensus on national goals and objectives in space and achieve greater stability in both objectives and related resource commitments.
-- Recognize the unavoidable interdependence of government and industry, not a relationship in which industry is an intrusion to be avoided, an interference or displacement of appropriate government objectives, or a competitor for the control and use of scarce resources.
-- Reach agreement on areas where the government will not compete. Develop processes for assuring this, and remedies for correction if it occurs.
-- Define government's responsibilities and obligations as a partner. Most would agree government should recognize a business's "right to fail," but government should also define the measures it will take to avoid contributing to space businesses failure by its own actions in the partnership, including the extent of remedies if failure occurs.
-- Recognize the continuing government role in support of basic technology and research, especially in high risk areas, by maintaining expertise and facilities in all scientific fields bearing upon activity in space. Specifically, the U.S. space industry should be viewed as a customer of government space research and technology programs, just as government is viewed as a customer of industrial design, development and production capabilities.
-- Establish through legislation innovative mechanisms to encourage (without subsidy) greater industry investment in

the development of space infrastructure that the Nation needs to reaffirm its leadership for both public and private missions.

Stability and predictability deserve special emphasis in encouraging greater private investment. There have been few more destructive impacts on private investment and public-private partnership than the constant changes in directions, funding, and goals in the U.S. Space programs that has occurred in the last decade. The Space Station program is a prime example. This Nation has spent over $1 billion to define what such a Station should look like and has involved the technical expertise and views of a vast number of users, reviewers, decision-makers, and advisors. At the technical design level, there is a strong commitment to the chosen configuration. Despite this, however, there are many who still talk about major "reviews" of the program or wholesale reconfigurations, or who still act as if the program were at the earliest conceptual design stages. At some point a commitment must be just that; if huge sums of funds, public and private, are not to be wasted, a program must either stop permanently or be given the support it needs to proceed apace. At some point, caution becomes merely vacillation, and leadership is lost.

Ironically, in the long view, it matters little what the initial configuration of the first Space Station will be. The capacity of space facilities that could result from private investment in a thriving U.S. space industry could eventually dwarf the initial capacity of the U.S. Space Station. The initial U.S. permanent manned presence is simply a seed for subsequent private efforts. What is important is to get that U.S. presence in place, and to do so through a stable, predictable effort. Hopefully, if no more time is wasted, it will do so before other nations follow the Soviet Union, who already has the space infrastructure to support a massive industrial effort in space.

However, if properly undertaken, the government-industry partnership approach can lead to industry investment and involvement in a wide spectrum of future space activities. Starting with relatively smaller and less complicated possibilities such as small launch vehicles, large-scale U.S. space business can be expected to evolve, such as:

-- On-orbit technical support services (e.g., payload maintenance, changeout, and repair);
-- On-orbit utilities (e.g., space power);

-- Major space transportation capabilities and services (launch vehicles, orbital re-entry vehicles, orbital maneuvering and transfer vehicles, upper stages);

-- Accommodation, recreation, health, and life support (the beginnings of permanent presence beyond an initial Space Station);

-- "As delivered" R&D facilities, missions, and services (e.g., turn-key facilities, "pay for data" science missions); and

-- Space-related ground facilities and services, including the processing, analysis, and distribution of remote sensing data.

SUMMARY

In the U.S. and other space-faring nations, space activity has, with a few exceptions, been an enterprise largely dominated by government. The reasons which have given rise to extensive government involvement will continue, dictating the need for close cooperation between industry and government if industry is to assume a significant role. Furthermore, in the long term, it may not be possible for any nation to sustain leadership in space without strong cooperation between government and industry. Long term economic development of space will eventually require the presence of numerous space platforms, new satellites of all kinds, and new ground support facilities. Such a vision is likely beyond the scale of what any government could support alone, and certainly beyond the scope of what it should support alone, just as an aeronautics industry of the scope or scale we know it today is beyond what government alone could or should have established or supported. But it is not beyond what the U.S., with the strongest private sector in the world, can achieve through an appropriate partnership between government and industry.

In such a partnership, the government should provide minimal and responsible oversight and regulation, support basic and responsive R&D and encourage large scale, independent private investment and involvement for infrastructure, products, and services. The role of the private sector should be to provide a range of goods and services required to generate commerce in and from space and to permit comfortable, efficient, and growing activities in space. Cooperation and commitment are the essential attributes of such a partnership.

This cooperative concept will provide the opportunity for eventual large scale and independent economic activity. As such, it may be the only way to reduce dramatically the fundamental costs of access and work in space and to maintain U.S. leadership in the continuing world-wide fiscal climate facing the space-faring world for the foreseeable future. If we commit to this transition in the right way, the opportunity is clearly there. The enabling observation is that the choice is not government *or* industry. The choice is to find ways for government and industry commitment to constructively work together for mutual benefit, or to abandon space leadership to those nations which will, and in some cases are today, making such commitments. Properly undertaken, there is no fundamental reason why U.S. private industry cannot be encouraged to accelerate economic activity in space for the benefit of all sectors. In so doing, we can bring a strong industrial role to an activity which has historically been largely dominated by government.

PART FOUR

Conclusions: Putting It All Together

Coming from different backgrounds, reflecting different perspectives, the essays in this volume present a panoply of insights and reflections on the current state of the U.S. civilian space program. If there is a single underlying theme among the authors, it is clearly a strong belief in the importance of the space program to the Nation, a common concern that all is not well with the program in its current state, and a conviction that the U.S. could better achieve public objectives in space even given the constrained Federal budgets likely to endure for the foreseeable future.

The final chapters seek to pull together the wisdom and sense of future directions which emerge from this "reconsideration" of our civilian space policy. Garry D. Brewer is a policy scientist and professor in the Yale University School of Organization and Management. He views the organization of NASA, and the history of the civilian space program -- both the triumphs and the tragedies -- through a series of "lenses" intended to clarify why NASA the institution behaves as it does. Drawing upon the concepts of organization theory, history, psychology, economics, political philosophy, psychiatry and ecology, Brewer shows how organizations that have achieved remarkable goals sometimes find it exceedingly hard to adjust to a drastically changed environment.

Some will find this assessment critical of NASA's senior management; others may find it an intriguing "explanation" for why the agency has historically placed so much emphasis on large, highly-visible projects such as the Space Shuttle and the Space Station which are vulnerable to major shifts in political sentiment or to exigencies such as the Federal budget deficit and the Gramm-Rudman-Hollings legislation.

The final chapter argues for more open and critical appraisals of the program, the policies which shape its directions, and ultimately the extent to which it contributes to the public good. The Editor and Professor Ronald Brunner of the University of Colorado Political Science Department suggest an agenda for future space policy research. The authors are convinced that it is time to establish a truly independent space policy community in the United States and to encourage wider participation in the process of setting policy for the program. Space is too important for the policy to be determined only by those who staff the federal agencies, including the oversight and review organizations in the Congress and the Executive Office of the President.

The U.S. has for the most part operated under a paradigm developed during Apollo. Times have changed dramatically since then, yet the vision of what the Nation might do in space, and the ways to do it, have not been updated to conform to the political and international landscape of the nineties. It is time to "reconsider" our space policies. It is time to recognize that "space is more than a place" -- space is a symbolic representation of what the United States will seek to achieve in the decades and centuries to follow. To choose wisely, the public must first understand the choices.

Chapter 10

PERFECT PLACES:
NASA AS AN IDEALIZED INSTITUTION

Garry D. Brewer

PERFECTION NEVER EXISTS IN REALITY BUT ONLY IN OUR
DREAMS AND, IF WE ARE FOOLISH ENOUGH TO THINK SO, IN
THE PAST.
DR. RUDOLPH DREIKURS

To "reconsider" something, such as space policy, logic demands
that there have been forethought. In my case, I am quick to
admit, there is not much to reconsider. I know precious little
about NASA or space policy. What I bring to the discussion is
twenty years of experience as a policy scientist who has worked to
understand and improve complex human institutions devoted to
political and economic development, urban renewal planning,
handicapped children, the command and control of strategic
nuclear forces, and, most recently, energy and other natural
resource and environmental problems. The consistent motivation
and common thread are my concerns about and fascination for
complex systems that do not perform well.

Indeed, the main reason I was invited to comment is because
several who know space policy and NASA very well believe this
once perfect institution is troubled and needs help from any
quarter and by all means possible.

Perhaps a fresh, outsider's perspective could shed new light?
On this good chance, I risk describing what I see. On the off
chance a different light can reveal nothing new, slight harm will
be done. And in any event, the little I know about NASA and

space means that I can speak my mind without particular preconceptions or prior commitments.[1]

Other contributors to this volume amply compensate for my specific substantial weaknesses. Indeed, this collection of experiences and talent has generated a stimulating and provocative array of ideas. I was solidly struck, in reading chapters of this volume and discussing them with their authors and with others, by everyone's deep feelings about the National Aeronautics and Space Administration. No one is ambivalent, and its harshest critics truly love the place.

Trying to account for all of this book's contributions, or even to summarize a few of its details, is quite impossible, so I did not try. What did occur to me repeatedly as I became immersed in the subject, was a general theme, with several specific elaborations.

The theme is that of *perfect places,* or *idealized institutions.* The six variants are based on how different disciplines and professionals might see and describe one perfect place: the National Aeronautics and Space Administration. These descriptive acts propose elements of a much needed, more thorough and continuing, analysis into the causes and nature of NASA's general condition as reflected in its many specific problems.

PERFECT PLACES

What do CBS, General Motors, the Bank of America, the U.S. Naval Academy, Yale University, and the horse cavalry have in common with NASA?

Each at some time or another came close to being the best organization human beings could create to accomplish selected goals. If not the best or perfect, they were nearly so. . .close enough. Ironically this very success ensured their eventual demise. In retrospect, the seeds of failure were sown with each success. We need to understand idealized institutions generally to come to better terms with NASA -- a specific and troubled perfect place.[2]

Success reinforces lessons that eventually become obsolete or even harmful. Only rarely in an institution's history can its surrounding environment be ignored, controlled, or flouted. News from the outside provides crucial cues for institutional adaptation and evolution. CBS was blessed with the genius of Edward R. Murrow, until his lessons hardened into dogma no one dared doubt. General Motors and the Bank of America once controlled their respective markets and enjoyed remarkable success, until changing world events proved each to be unresponsive, brittle, and poorly adapted. NASA perfected itself in the reality of Apollo, but that success is past and the lessons from it are now obsolete, not to be flouted.

Perfection stifles dissent, but dissent is the oxygen of all human institutions. Correcting and improving operations as circumstances change requires that someone step forward. But stepping forward in an idealized institution too often proves risky. Dissent becomes equated with disloyalty or with personal incapacity. Dissatisfaction is deviant, a truth many subordinates learn and later enact as so much sycophancy.

It took a Larry Tisch to shock CBS to the changing realities of high finance and the media in the 1980s. Ross Perot failed with a similar message at General Motors, but earned a huge bonus to keep quiet. In the late 1960s, Admiral Hyman P. Rickover brought the U.S. Naval Academy kicking and screaming into the 20th century by a steady stream of acid criticism directed at its curriculum and graduates. The Bank of America and Yale present stories in progress with endings still unknown -- quite unlike the horse cavalry, whose fate was sealed by machine gun and tank.[3]

Unfortunately, it seems to require the shock of heavy cannon to loosen dissent in a perfect place. Criticism is conveniently tamed. To be critical at all one must play by the rules, and team play is rule number one. Frankness and integrity are often sacrificed out of fear of becoming the messenger shot for bearing bad news.

Righteousness often leads members of idealized institutions to reinforce their "perfect" view of the world and their rightful place within it. The variety of possible views and versions of the world thus boils down to just one: the party line. In the extreme, the party line may even overpower ethical and legal considerations. If one is right, any means is valid and no need to ask questions about it. But, should one dare raise questions, retribution is certain and swift, beginning with being labeled by the in-group as poorly informed, weak, stupid or evil. Such classification reinforces the in-group's norms at the same time as it limits the possibilities for the existence of different values and views of the world.

These general characteristics of perfect places may not hold in every case, although their coincidence is seldom surprising. Nor are their consequences, which include flawed decision making, self deception, introversion and a diminished curiosity about the world outside the perfect place.[4] In extreme examples, as many "whistle blowers" could attest, intolerance and persecution also occur.

Those locked into perfect places have trouble seeing and reacting to flawed practices and failing performance -- problems an outsider might not mistake. Indeed, to this outsider at least, NASA and the space policy it carries out seem flawed and may even be failing. But rather than arguing the point, these matters need to be opened up, for instance to the scrutiny different outsiders and disciplinary perspectives afford.

The following sketches portray NASA as professionals from demography, history, economics, political science, psychiatry, and ecology might see it. None of the sketches is complete or definitive. The main idea for doing them is to illuminate NASA from unusual angles and with different hues to see what parts of it need closer attention, and by whom. A secondary idea is to suggest how one might compose the individual sketches into a richer whole picture. Ultimately, I hope this exercise assists those who care about and who are responsible for NASA -- an organization once as nearly perfect as any human beings could create.

DEMOGRAPHY

There are not very many people between the ages of forty-five and fifty-five in America. This Depression era and World War II fact is easily overlooked, which is regrettable. In the next ten to fifteen years, the managerial talent and professional leadership required to run America's institutions must be found within the small numbers of this cohort. Failing to do so will mean increasing pressure to search elsewhere -- for foreign sources, for untested younger people in the abundant thirty-five to forty-five age range, or for other unusual prospects.

This leadership succession problem facing the country hits NASA almost immediately and with incredible force. One-quarter of the top and middle management of NASA is currently eligible for voluntary retirement and within five years that proportion will exceed three-quarters.[5] No modern institution, especially one demanding so many technical and organizational skills of its managers and leaders as NASA, could survive such a hemorrhage undamaged. Taken alone, the threat is serious enough, but considered in the broader context of across-the-board increased demand for highly skilled human talent, the matter becomes critical.

Replenishment of NASA's ranks will not be easy nor will it mimic historical patterns. Foreign talent will undoubtedly become more evident, something already forecast in the Bromley/Packard report, but this would have happened at NASA anyway as space science, information, and business generally became more international.[6] Now it must happen faster, unless another U.S. national talent pool can be tapped. Some among the unusually young will have a splendid opportunity to lead, although their inexperience may prove risky. I cannot imagine a large proportion of NASA's leadership being so entrusted. And that constraint points toward a likelier source for regeneration: the military.

The armed services retire most of their officers after twenty years in uniform, when they are between forty and fifty years old, the exact cohort NASA must restock. Furthermore, in the last two decades the military has lavished advanced training and graduate education on its career officers, and much of this has been in fields NASA clearly needs most. Finally, the military culture is notorious for its capacity to create and sustain the party line, which is precisely what NASA needs least but what out of habit it may seek.

Unusual prospects are not so readily identified, although the problem of leadership degeneracy in truly rich, family-run businesses is suggestive.[7] Under present circumstances going outside the NASA "family" of engineers and technicians to employ different sorts of professionals in leadership positions may allow new views and values to infuse the agency. Lawyers, accountants, and business people historically perform such a role, a melancholy prospect for some scientists and engineers who already yearn for the good old days.[8]

HISTORY

Institutions both create and react to events. Taken altogether, such events provide a record or history whose careful telling and honest appraising may allow one to distinguish fact from fiction, myth from reality. In perfect places in serious trouble, making these distinctions is often the first action needed to set matters straight.

Getting straight with history can be a painful experience. The saga of the tribe, any tribe, transmits both the norms and the aspirations of a binding culture. Unique events and personalities matter, but typically take on larger-than-life proportion as the saga is retold and unbalanced by dwelling on the good parts and skipping over the bad.

In time, only the most tough-minded and skillful historian can redress a balance while reminding the tribe of its true relationships to its surroundings -- its effects on and reactions to the world at large. Criticism is essential if the tribe and its culture are to evolve and thereby survive.

Historians help transmit the culture, but they are equally able to criticize and assist in its evolution. Truth telling, even though it clashes with the conventional wisdom of the oft told saga, is crucial even if, and usually especially when, most unwelcome. Alex Roland's chapter in this volume ranks as such "truth telling" in my view. The measure of its unwelcomeness he will soon discover, but I bet that before the shock of Challenger few in the NASA tribe heeded him or basic messages of the sort he tells us here. And if NASA is a perfect place in demise, they probably still will not. In some cases, such critics can become targets for the hostile release of corporate insecurities and pent up frustrations. Let's hope this will not happen here.

ECONOMICS

The national security origins of NASA, its personnel and programs, parallel to a large extent those of civilian nuclear power, another collection of activities where common concepts from economics have not applied, have been misconstrued, or have been ignored. At some point, as Molly Macauley reminds us in this book, the dismal science takes its toll. Let us consider costs, both sunk and opportunity, and investments, both political and lumpy.

Sunk costs ought to be ignored according to pure economic dicta: What's been spent is spent, so forget it. The difficulty comes when economic purity is contaminated by political realities, including the egos and reputations of those who made the decisions and did the spending. Sunk costs in NASA's world are to be defended or rationalized, for to do otherwise would admit the error of past decisions. And if a place is perfect, error is impossible.

By similar reasoning the expected change in NASA's cast of characters might allow economics to count more heavily, because the new leadership will not be so bound by past decisions. It is more likely, however, that present and emerging economic realities outside of NASA will simply force whoever ends up being in charge to change the old fashioned ways. As David Moore and the Congressional Budget Office argue so convincingly, budget constraints make serious choices imperative for NASA in the 1990s.[9]

Past decisions resulted in investments both large and lumpy and, here too, economics and politics got tangled up. A proper aerospace program is measured in billions, not millions, of dollars. The hardware is expensive, but the political reality is at least as determinative of the cost of programs. Getting a big program approved takes the expenditure of about as much political capital as a small one. In addition big programs provide more jobs, press coverage, and votes, thereby ensuring against cutbacks and termination. The economic costs *are* the political benefits. Big programs mean big business.

But big also means limiting commitment to one or, at best, a few courses of action. There is not enough money or talent to do otherwise. This refers to what economists call opportunity costs. That is, what else might have been accomplished with the resources spent on the one-big-project? An even more refined version of this question relates to NASA. What other *ongoing* responsibilities were stretched out, neglected, or sacrificed to sustain the one-big-project?

Economics plays a role as big investments often become lumpy ones. Years may pass before a space program's thousands of pieces finally come together, to succeed or not. There are few opportunities to sense and correct errors threatening the total system. Worse yet, if there is only one game in town, even the hint of failure cannot be tolerated. Failing big thus becomes a distinct possibility with only a single, cosmic throw of the dice.

Now consider incentives. When someone borrows $50 thousand from a bank and later defaults, he loses his house and car and is forever branded unworthy of credit. But if someone borrows and defaults on $50 million, the bank makes that person a partner! Big in this sense ensures against individual failure and spreads blame around to many others. Default is unacceptable, and the bigger the loan, the more this is so. Cost overruns and program stretch-outs are often motivated by comparably bizarre factors. Economists worry about perverse incentives and have a trove of ways to help set them straight. But ours is a space program where cost overruns are expected.[10] Where is the 1980s equivalent of an Ike, who was known to fire top officials for exceeding a budget?

Costs and benefits are the literal "stuff" of economics, but they assume new meanings or do not apply when swept up in a political process. If discounted net benefits exceed costs, then an investment is economical. But there are some catches. What discount rates apply? Whose costs and benefits? A high discount rate means the future matters less than if a low rate applies. Is NASA a one-year, ten-year, or fifty-year payback opportunity? The question seems never to have been considered. Costs and benefits to society over the long haul are not the same as costs and benefits to one's political constituents, figured between now and next election.   Indeed, a prevalent political cost-benefit calculation goes as follows: Maximize benefits in the short term for one's constituents while displacing costs to the future to be paid by "the public" at large. The calculation, although cynical, helps account for the behavior of many elected officials. And for top NASA management, about to retire en masse, a one-year time frame seems quite likely. So much for long range "Goals for NASA."

Now consider the surrounding economic environment, including trends in the general climate. The appearance and reality of increasing economic opportunity allow less stringent standards to guide policies and discipline programs. Price is no object. Borrow or charge it.   There are no limits.   NASA's conception, development and existence have all occurred under such circumstances. But the reality of huge budget deficits funded by foreign creditors soon enough must overshadow the contrived, election year appearances of business as usual. And when that happens, the dismal fact that NASA is an expensive, but discretionary, item in the national budget may prove painful indeed.   And the pain may be inflicted automatically by the remorseless machinery of Gramm-Rudman-Hollings.

POLITICS, ANCIENT AND MODERN

Plato worried about "Who would watch the guardians themselves?", one of civilization's earliest frets about having to depend on specialized elites. Concern persists, and for good, understandable reasons.

At NASA one of those reasons is the "climate of opinion," in Alex Roland's apt turn of phrase. And that climate is rather like San Diego's: Perfect, until you live there for a while and have to do more than go to the beach. Groupthink, the party line, and "We know best" tell the tale.

Groupthink happens when a collection of decision makers spreads total responsibility around indiscriminately. No one wants to take the rap if matters go awry, so no one takes the lead or any chances. The lowest common denominator prevails -- both in choices and in the choosers.[11]

The party line we already know about. No perfect place is complete without one. The party line allows today's Platonic guardians to talk to themselves. And talk, and talk, and talk they do, especially if relations among themselves are fragile. The party line reassures individual confidence and bolsters collective righteousness. What is happening everywhere else hardly matters at all -- at least for a while.

"We know best" shows up in lots of ways, not the least of which is in the language the party-line groupthinkers use. If you do not know and use the language, then you obviously do not know best . . . what to do, why it should be done, and how to do it. But, as most contributions to this book suggest, *what, why,* and *how* are all up for grabs at NASA right now.

Political observers closer at hand than Plato worry about precisely these conditions: times when direction, reason, and means in human affairs simultaneously come into question. Such occurrences may lead to "risky shifts," where id displaces ego as a basis for action. The risky shift may occur when uncertainty about what to do is multiplied by repeated failures of routine choices to produce satisfactory outcomes. Panic is also sometimes evident. Consequently, failing-big is nearly assured, because an impulsive commitment to an old vision blocks out any appreciation of new realities.

The introversion of NASA's elite has happened at a time when the public's mood is unsettled and very hard to divine. No one gives the average guy on the street high marks for knowing a celestial technical best: space station, go to Mars, or cooperate with the Russians? In fact the guy on the street, recent scientific surveys gloat, hardly knows where Paris is, much less what TDRS or Hubble might bode. But the ease with which public attentions were captured and focused on the Challenger tragedy or on medical wastes washed ashore on last summer's beaches says that the average Joe or Jane does not need to know technical specifics to be personally frightened and generally distrustful of "They" who should have been doing their jobs as well as Plato's guardians, but who obviously were not.

The bomber gap, missile gap, window of vulnerability, and Sputnik each served as potent slogans to galvanize, focus, and move human passions and attentions. It hardly mattered that each slogan and its supporting rhetoric barely reflected reality. Politics involves perception and vision, which are subject to manipulation and control. In general, NASA sells its vision to the politicians and the public, but only NASA has the technical expertise to question this vision. Regrettably, it also has little incentive to do so. Having a near monopoly on information and appraisal allows NASA to operate unhindered by independent and knowing criticism.

166

If only the complex operational realities were compatible with the simple, sustaining, public vision. But they aren't, as Challenger clearly revealed.

What might any of this mean for NASA in years to come? It is very hard, and foolish, to offer firm estimates. But it is much easier to imagine a world very different from the glorious one which gave us Apollo and a man on the Moon. The innocent clarity of purpose, the relatively easy and economically painless public consent, and the technical confidence of twenty years ago are gone and will probably never occur again. The barnstorming era is over. Trying to recreate those by-gone moments by sloganeering, frightening, or appealing to humankind's mystical needs for exploration and conquest seems somehow futile considering all that has happened since Jack Kennedy set the nation on course to the Moon.

PSYCHIATRY

A psychiatrist is trained to analyze intensely individual human beings. The psychiatric perspective can produce insights into one's self and various life situations, especially where the self has failed to be integrated into or rationalized with circumstances. The failure to acknowledge changing circumstances and the setting of unrealistic motivational goals are two common problems a psychiatrist learns to sense and treat. Death, for example, is an inevitable life change few cope with easily and a circumstance where a psychiatric perspective often proves helpful.[12]

Just as every life must end, so it is with every war and most other human endeavors.[13] One may resist the prospect for a time, or deny it manically or in depressed rage, but inevitability rules. So why this dreary line of thought? What does it matter for NASA and the larger human project in space?

It matters quite a bit I believe. It matters because those in perfect places do not want shrinks, and the nuttier things become, the more they are not wanted. It matters when realistic appraisals of self-in-situation rarely occur or are manifestly delusional. And it matters most of all when every signal from the world outside shouts "change," or implores "decide," but the individual or institution plows resolutely along. And that, in short, is what NASA is doing. Criticism and doubts simply reinforce the will to impose the party line vision on the environment, not to reconsider it.

As any good psychoanalyst knows, a reasonably healthy personality is defined functionally according to several characteristics.   Central and of high priority is a capacity to provide realistic appraisals of one's self in varying circumstances so as to solve problems effectively. Solving in this sense is not a black or white matter but rather one of degree. Sometimes just coping with a problem is good enough, most especially so if today's small success lays the groundwork for more substantial ones in the future. The setting of realistic and attainable goals is implicated here, something neither NASA leadership nor their political superiors seem able to do. Or, as Casey Stengel put it: "If you don't know where you're going, you may end up somewhere else."

Quite as high a priority must be assigned to completing acts once begun and not drawing them out. Terminating most anything in human affairs is dreadfully difficult. It is also absolutely critical if one's creative powers are to flourish. Often there must be destruction before there can be creation, where destruction means ending something to free up time and other resources to make something brand new.

The concept is of course familiar to economists. Bankruptcy, including restructuring debt, redeploying human and other capital resources, and refocusing on feasible corporate goals, are common means by which these general, cyclical processes operate.

In only slightly altered form such a conception is also commonplace to ecologists, all of whom appreciate the importance of nutrient and other elemental recycling. The basic idea is less familiar to others not so well tuned to life's complexities and cycles. Other ecological ideas are also worth considering, despite their apparently only superficial relevance to NASA and space.

ECOLOGY

As far removed from rockets and other exotic space paraphernalia as ecologists seem to be, the ecological perspective is essential. Take the idea in its broadest sense as systems in interaction, including their human components.

We have had inklings of this necessary added dimension. Just recall the incredible power over human imagination one photograph of Earth from space possessed. Talk about a "vision;" it inspired a movement! Or focus hard on the fact that human beings can exist in space only with respect for the integrity and deep understanding of the complexity in life systems. There is no choice, just as there are no convenience stores on the Moon.

Think about building systems so adaptive and resilient (root concepts in ecology) that errors both probable and totally unknown might be accommodated or even managed. Wheelon's wise commentary in this volume converts readily from his language as an experienced engineer to that of a committed environmentalist, as startling as that may seem. Consider the equivalent meanings of key words and ideas he and a good ecologist might use.[14]

-- Resilience
-- Adaptation
-- Redundancy
-- Diversity

Resilience is the ability to spring back or to recover from misfortune or change. In living systems it also means the capability of withstanding shock without permanent damage.

Adaptation or *adaptive* is an adjustment to environmental conditions or the modification of an organism to fit conditions of an environment better. Critical to adaptation are the needs to know about the status of and to harmonize with the conditions of one's surroundings.

Redundancy is an overflowing, an excess of what is necessary or normal. In extreme instances, redundancy may be needless or inefficient. On the positive side, redundancy is a strategy for realizing resilience and adaptation by providing multiple means of achieving an objective despite internal breakdowns and external shocks.

Diversity is a condition of being or having differences -- a desirable state usually attained by increasing the variety of components or stock materials in living systems.[15]

These are not just ecological and biological concepts, they are valuable ways of thinking about social and decision processes, particularly in contrast to the mechanistic concepts and metaphors that dominate the thought, language, and action at NASA.[16]

Wheelon's chapter is as intelligible to an ecologist as it is to an engineer. He seems to be searching for different ways to make sense of a new reality defiant of rigid categories and rational tidiness. He opens with the idea of redundancy, but then stresses its most limited meaning: having more than one of something to accomplish a task, e.g., two lungs, two eyes, and so forth. Perhaps the term's more central meaning of excessive or overflowing leads him to replace it with a more vigorous concept of resilience, which he quickly applies as a being a good result of diversity. And as his discussion proceeds, additional concepts from ecology are brought to bear with good and clarifying effect.

Diversity and redundancy, along with other mainstay ideas such as adaptive, evolutionary, and interdependent, vividly capture aspects of space by focusing on human needs and aspirations, while simultaneously highlighting biological constraints. The ecological paradigm is a powerful complement to the narrower technical ones that have so far prevailed.

Ecology presents more general lessons for NASA staff and leaders to consider. In complex biological systems in which human acts both cause and are acted on by various systemic components, no one usually knows enough to pre-engineer anything, especially if the time frame extends to decades. Ecology, nonetheless, provides concepts and guidance for coping with systems no one understands very well: The first lesson is that no one can know enough to plan ahead very far or with much certainty. The second lesson is that surprises happen, and may overpower anyone's well meant plans. And the third is that perfect places do not last for long, if they ever existed at all.[17]

A pre-engineered mega project is a manifestation of perfect place thinking. In ecology, perfect places do not exist. There is always disequilibrium and continuous striving for something better.

NASA stands for technological hubris. It thus resists any questioning of goals or means and the assumptions on which these are based. The consequences are everywhere harmful, to the society and to NASA itself. New perspectives, associated with new ways of thinking and more fitting concepts, are urgently needed to account for present and new realities and to invigorate the human project in space. Different disciplines and knowledge from many different life experiences must be enlisted in this quest.

NASA is no longer a perfect place. It is deeply troubled and needs new ways of thinking, new people, and new means to come to terms and cope with social, economic, and political environments as challenging and harsh as deep space itself. These sketches are provided as points of departure.

THE ROLES OF CRITICAL ANALYSES

By now few could doubt the need for ongoing, thorough, and honest appraisal of NASA and the policy it carries out. Diagnoses from any reasonable perspective converge in agreement that major rethinking and redirecting are long overdue. Even without new thought or guidance, NASA must continue to change. External circumstances allow it no choice. The central question is whether the changes will be anticipated and channeled toward positive ends or whether they will "just happen," with consequences no one either expects or particularly wants.

The answer to this question is neither foregone nor obvious. The pathologies of perfect places are especially evident and strong in NASA's case. Overcoming them is a first order of business, for NASA's new leadership, in the years immediately ahead.

And this business must emphasize analysis: the examination, dissection, and resolution of the complex entity we call NASA, including its elements and their relations.

Often when analyzing complex organizations that are not working well or as intended, it is important to stimulate new visions and to provoke the asking of different questions. Doing so is hard work whose payoff sometimes occurs as a new strategy and different plans of action. The points of stimulating and provoking are to reveal outmoded and unrealistic assumptions and to replace them with valid ones that may lead to success. But the assumptions in any event must be made explicit so that they can be tested against reality, and changed when it becomes obvious to do so.

For example, the wishful thinking driving both thought and action in the case of the space station needs to be offset by a quite different set of more fearful assumptions: What if the federal budget is slashed? What if usual Congressional support for NASA programs declines or shifts to other priorities? What if the American public begins to be more excited by the danger of ozone holes than by the possibility of putting a man on Mars? What if national security requirements in space cannot be pursued simultaneously with civilian ones -- because of cost, inadequate talent, or for other imaginable reasons? Or if there were fewer demands for national security, where would we put the nation's treasure?

Imagine, for a moment, a very different vision of man in space. Until now, Buck Rogers and other barnstorming swashbucklers filled the imagination when thought of outer space crossed our minds. The Washington cliche, "There are no bucks without Buck Rogers," a political explanation for space expenditures, reflects the same vision. Buck, Captain Kirk, Spock, and the others are always heading away, ever farther from Earth. Our appreciation for them is never more than by proxy. But what if -- the analyst's canonical question -- the visual standpoint were to shift, so that our imaginations were anchored in near space but were looking back toward Earth, our first, last, and only frontier? The role of humankind in space is thus reconceived to include *all of humanity, on Earth, surviving together, in space.* Hardly a vicarious thought! And it might even provide a public rationale for NASA to survive.[18]

The role of analysis and analysts in NASA's reinvention must include fundamental and creative thinking of this sort. The objective of discovering new ways of thinking and acting is as essential as predicting the likely course of familiar thoughts or acts long in progress. Likewise, the need to appraise ongoing actions openly, honestly, independently, and continuously takes on high priority. The several roles analysis must perform reduce to three simple actions: transmit, criticize, and create.

And so far, transmissions from NASA seem uncritical and hardly creative. Indeed, to many people they have become barely readable or simply garbled.

NOTES

1. Several knowledgeable colleagues read and commented constructively on an earlier version of this chapter, and I am much in their debt. Radford Byerly and Ronald Brunner of the University of Colorado and Alice Eichold, a NASA Fellow in Yale University's School of Forestry and Environmental Studies (of all places), contributed perspectives and expertise I found most compelling.

2. The specific task has been ably started, albeit ingenuously, by Richard P. Feynman, "Mr. Feynman Goes to Washington," *Engineering & Science* [the alumni magazine of CalTech] (Fall 1987): 6-22.

3. The bank story is widely known. Gary Hector, *Breaking the Bank: The Decline of BankAmerica* (Boston: Little, Brown, 1988). But symptoms of Yale's demise are just appearing. James R. Norman, "Days of Rage at Yale B-School," *Business Week* (December 12, 1988): 36-37. The horse cavalry persisted well past its useful lifetime, a trait of many idealized institutions. Edward L. Katzenbach, "The Horse Cavalry in the Twentieth Century," *Public Policy*, vol. 8 (1958): 120-49.

4. Lloyd S. Etheredge, *Can Governments Learn?* (Elmsford, NY: Pergamon Press, 1985).

5. Personnel Analysis and Evaluation Division, *The Civil Service Work Force* (Washington, D.C.: NASA Headquarters, 1987), p. 65.

172

6. White House Science Council, Panel on the Health of U.S. Colleges and Universities, *A Renewed Partnership* (Washington, D.C.: OSTP, February 1986). This is updated in National Research Council, "Foreign Engineers: Assets or Liabilities?" *News Report*, vol. 38, no. 2 (February 1988): 11-14.

7. Ford Motor Company is illustrative. The myth is called to question in Keith Sward, *The Legend of Henry Ford* (New York: Atheneum, 1972); and it is demolished in Lee Iacocca, *Iacocca* (New York: Bantam, 1984), where special animus is heaped on Henry Ford II.

8. Freeman Dyson, *Disturbing the Universe* (N.Y.: Harper & Row, 1979). "The fun went out of the business [reference to Los Alamos]. The adventurers, the experimenters. . .were driven out, and the accountants and managers took control."

9. Moore in this volume, and U.S. Congress, Congressional Budget Office, *The NASA Program in the 1990s and Beyond* (Washington: GPO, May 1988).

10. For example, the GAO has done a series of reports on cost overruns and delays in NASA missions. See (a) Space Exploration/Cost, Schedule, and Performance of NASA's Galileo Mission to Jupiter, GAO/NSIAD-88-138FS. (b) Space Exploration/NASA's Deep Space Missions are Experiencing Long Delays, GAO/NSIAD-88-128BR. (c) Space Exploration/Cost, Schedule, and Performance of NASA's Magellan Mission to Venus, GAO/NSIAD-88-130FS. (d) Space Exploration/Cost, Schedule, and Performance of NASA's Ulysses Mission to the Sun, GAO/NSIAD-88-129FS. (All Washington, D.C.: U.S. General Accounting Office, May, 1988).

11. Irving Janis, *Groupthink* (Boston: Houghton Mifflin, 1983 ed.).

12. Ernest Becker, *The Denial of Death* (New York: The Free Press, 1973).

13. Fred Charles Ikle, *Every War Must End* (New York: Columbia University Press, 1971), combines historical, political, and terminal views in a most instructive fashion for present needs.

14. Robert M. *May, Stability and Complexity in Model Ecosystems* (Princeton, N.J.: Princeton University Press, 1973).

15. Gordon H. Orians, "Diversity, Stability, and Maturity in Natural Ecosystems," in W.H. Van Dobben and R.H. Lowe-McConnell, eds., *Unifying Concepts in Ecology* (The Hague: W. Junk, 1975): 139-50.

16. Richard R. Nelson, "Intellectualizing about the Moon-Ghetto Metaphor" *Policy Sciences*, vol. 5, no. 4 (December 1974): 375-414.

17. Carl Walters, *Adaptive Management of Renewable Resources* (New York: Macmillan, 1986); and National Research Council, *Ecological Knowledge and Environmental Problem-Solving* (Washington, D.C.: National Academy Press, 1986), are essential reading.

18. This thought has been stunningly illustrated in Kevin W. Kelley, ed. *The Home Planet* (Reading, Mass.: Addison-Wesley and Moscow: Mir Publishers, 1988). "Once a photograph of the Earth, taken from *the outside*, is available. . .a new idea as powerful as any in history will be let loose." Fred Hoyle, 1948 [from the jacket cover].

Chapter 11

FUTURE DIRECTIONS FOR SPACE
POLICY RESEARCH

Radford Byerly, Jr., and Ronald D. Brunner

THE DOGMAS OF THE QUIET PAST ARE INADEQUATE TO THE
STORMY PRESENT.

LINCOLN

The preceding essays have raised many issues. In this
concluding chapter we step back from the individual essays, draw
on our own experience, and consider the lessons and implications
for the future of space policy research. In particular we (1)
contend that the Apollo Paradigm, as a general way of seeing
space policy, is increasingly obsolete, (2) suggest some specific
priority research problems in a Post-Challenger Paradigm, and (3)
recommend the broadening of such future research through the
use of experience from other policy areas and the emerging
discipline of public policy.[1]

THE BASIC LESSON

In our judgment, many of the difficulties described in these
essays stem from a complex of assumptions, often taken for
granted, that was described in the Introduction to this volume as
the Apollo Paradigm. That paradigm has become increasingly
obsolete and counterproductive as a framework for research and
decision in civilian space policy.

The Apollo Paradigm emphasizes a vision that favors the selection of projects of a certain kind. Such favored projects are:

-- large, both in physical size and in complexity, and accordingly expensive;
-- pre-engineered according to a centralized plan, integrated with other projects, and thus vulnerable to the failure of any weak link; and
-- dependent upon long-term, stable, and focussed political support.

In the ecological metaphor advanced by Brewer, projects of this kind are increasingly less "fit" or "adaptive" as the social, economic, and political environment changes.

Consider the dependence on stable political support and how it affects the survivability of programs. Apollo probably did have broad consensus support at its start but the support withered: Apollo funding was brutally phased down even before the first man stepped on the Moon. As part of the current budget process an attempt is underway to force a go/no-go decision on the Space Station, with the hope that if the decision is to go ahead, there will be no further debate and the requested funds will be appropriated annually for the thirty-year life of the project. But our system of government does not work that way. In the era of Gramm-Rudman-Hollings the regular annual budget debates will be even more brutal because the need is to allocate cuts, not increments, of resources.

Even after development costs have been incurred, it will still be cheaper -- in terms of Federal dollar outlays -- to cancel than to continue. And because total operating costs will be larger than development costs, there will be repeated review of the worth of continuing. Therefore Space Station, a program that exemplifies the Apollo Paradigm, strongly depends on political support that may be difficult to sustain over several decades: It will be difficult during the construction period when expenses are high and there are few results to show, and it will be difficult when "permanent presence" becomes routinized and unexciting but operational costs remain high. In these respects the Apollo Paradigm does not contribute to a vigorous space program.

The Apollo Paradigm also de-emphasizes or ignores other criteria that have become increasingly necessary for "viable" projects:

-- appreciation of unpleasant contingencies that are overlooked in success-oriented planning, such as hardware failures, changing user needs, and emerging competition;
-- resilience or flexibility to respond to events that cannot be entirely predicted or controlled; and
-- renewal of the political consensus required to sustain a program.

Each of these can be expanded with an example.

First, consider the need to appreciate unpleasant contingencies such as hardware failures. There is a reasonable chance that there will be another Shuttle accident before Station is assembled,[2] but current plans assume that four orbiters will be available throughout the period. The Apollo Paradigm encourages such "success-oriented" plans. However, plans and results need to be evaluated realistically, explicitly, continuously, and at least partly independently in order to maintain their viability.

Flexibility is needed so that feedback from such evaluations or unexpected signals from the environment can be incorporated gracefully. The Apollo Paradigm sees flexibility as a negative characteristic to the extent that it makes a program vulnerable to interference or changes by OMB or Congress. The assumption is that potential budget cuts are more easily resisted if it can be argued that they would have a catastrophic impact on the target program.

The need to maintain a political consensus behind a project seems obvious, but the important thing is the strategy employed. James Webb -- next to John Glenn and John Kennedy perhaps the person most closely associated with the Apollo program -- recommended keeping the national interest in focus and measuring the degree to which programs are concurrent with the national interest by the support gathered.[3] If programs did not maintain support they were modified or abandoned. This was very different from the strategy employed for the Station: That is, the attempt to force a go/no-go decision (described above) and the earlier attempt to institutionalize support by giving a major role to five different NASA Centers. This splitting of responsibility complicated the internal politics and management of the program. Curiously, Webb might well reject the Apollo Paradigm, and not recognize it as related to his work.

The implication is that a new paradigm is needed for space policy and policy research. The Introduction suggests that this be called the Post-Challenger Paradigm, and that it supplement the vision of the Apollo Paradigm with more realistic analysis. Neither vision nor analysis alone is sufficient.

SPECIFIC PROBLEMS

A Post-Challenger Paradigm raises the priority of several current but relatively neglected problems, and provides a different perspective that may make these problems tractable.

(1) *Costs*, both annual and total, are more important in this era of unprecedented Federal deficits not yet under control. It is no longer reasonable to assume that escalating costs will be easily absorbed, or that costs will be discounted in favor of technical performance. If a project is allowed to exceed its budget, there will be large opportunity costs as other projects are postponed, curtailed, or cancelled; large political costs as political "chips" are expended to secure extra funds; or a reduction in program flexibility caused by mortgaging the future as was done in the case of the Tracking and Data Relay Satellite System (TDRSS).[4]

Traditionally the role of the political system has been to deliver the funds needed to carry out the vision of space exploration: Mission design was specified first and then costs were determined by the amount of money needed to achieve the desired design. The system (driven largely by Federal procurement regulations) has been sensitive to annual appropriation ceilings but insensitive to overall project costs.[5]

The problem is that the design of a science mission, for example, is typically determined by asking users "what do you need?" This generates a wish-list which is then used to justify building a large, expensive system to do many of the things on the list. (This preserves broad support in the user community.) To make cost a more significant criterion one must ask instead, "if you had a dollar, how would you spend it?" This very different question allows, indeed forces, fundamental consideration of alternatives for meeting needs.

Policy research is called for: How can we put incentives into the procurement system to hold down costs and get the most for each dollar invested? The Congress has tried caps through Gramm-Rudman-Hollings, and Moore has considered their potential impacts. Struthers has considered how both the Administration and Congress have promoted "commercialization" of space activities in part to reduce costs. However, it may be difficult to achieve the anticipated benefits of "commercializing" critical activities which the government will not allow to fail. For example, if the government is determined to build a Space Station then it cannot reasonably allow *critical* elements to be built commercially, if the definition of "commercial" includes some real risk. What other approaches might work?

(2) *Performance* is also increasingly important, and the criteria of performance are changing. NASA has a good record with respect to the ultimate technical performance of its missions but there is a disturbing tendency to defer delivery of results. Missions are taking longer and longer between initiation and culmination. Galileo began in 1976 but data from Jupiter will not be available before 1995. Station "began" in 1984 and the first element launch is planned for 1995 with complete assembly of Block I in 1998, and Block I is only a fraction of what was envisioned in 1984. The deferral of payoffs into the future discounts the present value of a mission, both politically and economically, which makes program support and funding more problematical.

In addition, "technical" criteria of success are becoming less important: It is not enough merely to fly hardware successfully; *de facto* standards will be set through competition, especially if users are allowed to choose. The fact that the Shuttle is a great technical success[6] and copied by the Soviets is less important than whether users believe that it can take their payloads into space reliably and efficiently, compared to the alternatives. One user, the U.S. Air Force, has decided that the Shuttle is not its vehicle of choice for many payloads,[7] and Giacconi has described in this volume how scientists want to be free to choose other launchers. In the beginning it was enough merely to get into space. But reliability and efficiency become more important once the uses of space have been demonstrated. The barnstorming era described by Roland cannot last forever.

Another performance criterion falling into disrepute is "space leadership." By itself "leadership" is directionless; if unqualified it allows others to set directions. In the past we were clearly leaders but others have caught up, in part because we deferred payoffs.

In summary, our space program has emphasized technical challenge and performance -- Oppenheimer's "sweetness" -- over real and solid utility. The policy research problem is to devise ways to stimulate and challenge the people in the program to achieve both technical improvement and cost-effective utility. Because the latter is more difficult, it could be even more challenging and stimulating.

(3) *Support for a manned space program* is broad and continuing, neither fragile nor intense in the general population. Opposition to specific manned activities arises when they are bungled or interfere with other activities. Nevertheless it seems that there has been a loss of nerve, a lack of faith in the popular support for manned space programs *per se*, and this doubt in turn leads program managers to overpromise.

The prime example is the Shuttle, which was overjustified as a cargo booster. This overjustification meant that science missions were forced to fly on Shuttle. Making this manned vehicle serve as our only launch provider and thus as the only way for science payloads to get to space harmed the overall program in three ways: Astronauts were put fatally at risk merely to launch cargos such as unmanned science missions and communications satellites; the Shuttle was overcommitted and faltered;[8] and a million pounds of science payloads were idled.[9]

A similar lack of faith in public support is manifest in the Station program which now offers something to large numbers of diverse users and contractors in many congressional districts. This is one way programs become large, complex, costly, slow-to-fruition, and inflexible.

The point is that a manned program might be justified on its own, without connecting it to other programs and activities. The research problem is to decide whether and how this might work. A low risk way to begin would be to stimulate a broad, open, informed, and vigorous debate on this question.

(4) *Large projects* take longer to develop, which means they may become technically obsolete before they are flown. In this way old technologies get locked into flight projects, as Wheelon and Giacconi each have described. This together with insensitivity to cost may make such large projects irrelevant or even counterproductive both to U.S. industrial competitiveness and to the education of the next generation of engineers and scientists.

Large-scale goals do not necessarily require large-scale, centralized projects. Some large-scale goals can be realized efficiently by small evolutionary steps which take advantage of feedback to delete unpromising alternatives and to develop the promising ones. In situations where we can neither predict nor control the future of a project nor the environment on which it depends, such an evolutionary approach is probably the best course.

There are assertions that the observed trend to larger science missions is inevitable, that it results from the nature of space science.[10] A research question: Is this true, or is the trend a result of budget and procurement policies, incentive structures, and other factors not directly related to space science per se? Projects like Station might be kept smaller by empowering users -- for example, by expanding the opportunity for them to advocate smaller projects that are quicker to fruition. More generally the questions are, what drives projects toward giantism in our system, and how can it be changed?

Some projects, such as a manned mission to Mars, are unavoidably large. A research question is how to modularize them so they can be accomplished effectively even if problems arise. Initially, modules may cost a little more in the short-run, but in the long-run might avoid the domino effect of costly failures rippling through a tightly integrated system. How much modularity is enough, and how can we achieve it?

(5) *Single-point failures* should be avoided where possible in programs as well as in physical systems. The decision to make Shuttle our sole launch vehicle put a large, unnecessary single-point failure mode into the U.S. space program. Similarly the decision to plan the Space Station so that it can be assembled and serviced only by Shuttle puts *the same* single-point failure mode into the Station program. There is a significant chance that a Shuttle accident will lose a Station assembly payload, and as of now there are no spares provided in the program plan. It is even possible that if certain assembly elements were lost, the partly-built Station could re-enter.

Another example is TDRSS. When our ground tracking stations are shut down the U.S. civilian space program will be relying largely on TDRSS to control spacecraft. Our ability to communicate with spacecraft that have degraded attitude control will be greatly reduced. And we will have reduced redundancy in the U.S. space program.

In each of these cases short-term budget considerations have been a major driver in the decision not to provide backups. If everything works as planned, the costs of backups are avoided. However, the aftermath of the Challenger accident showed that the costs of failure can be extremely large when there is no backup. Some redundancy is often efficient and effective.

In the recent past plans have assumed success, and when the inevitable failures occurred Congress has delivered the funds to fix the program or the program has simply suffered (as is the case of space science after Challenger). This was not always the case. In the early planetary program missions were typically planned in

182

pairs so that if one spacecraft failed the other could serve. As mission costs escalated this practice was dropped.

It may well be that the best decision is to tolerate the risks implicit in the decisions to build in such single-point failures, but the risks and costs should be openly debated -- these are not merely technical decisions. Research could inform such a debate.

The science community is well aware of this situation and has proposed approaches at least to mitigate it. The core program for planetary exploration is one example.[11] There are at least two kinds of research questions. The first has to do with risk tradeoffs, basically asking the question of when the risk of failure becomes too costly. As planetary missions become rarer, failure becomes a bigger risk to the community. The second kind of question asks why the system works as it does. What drives decisions to rely solely on Shuttle? Why are alternatives dismissed? Why is open debate avoided?

(6) *Competition* with our allies, not just the Soviet Union, is increasing and must be dealt with. Competition may directly and simply affect outcomes: For example, Ariane's effectiveness and aggressiveness may determine whether a commercial U.S. ELV industry survives. Competition may also compound other problems. For example, large projects may be too slow to adapt to competition. Thus the Europeans may learn what they need to know from our Station program, then develop an independent, low-cost alternative, leaving us with massive, expensive infrastructure in space and an institution needing lots of attention and support.

Foreign competition presents many intriguing research questions. The first is, what can we learn from our competitors? Our allies at least are quite open and we could learn how they operate. Second, are we willing to learn? That is, why can not or will not we adopt foreign practices or approaches that seem to work better than ours? Third, if we can't "join 'em," how can we "beat 'em"? That is, does our system have any underutilized strengths? Fourth, are there some areas in which we should yield to the economist's concept of comparative advantage and merely buy from foreigners? For example, when earth resource images are needed should we buy them from SPOT-Image and Soyuzkarta?

(7) *Efficiency* has been sought through centralization and integration (interdependence) of projects and through economies of scale (large size). Thus unwittingly our program has adopted

a Soviet model, vitiating the strengths of our system -- individual initiative, redundancy, and flexibility. The perverse result is that we have become less efficient. We need to learn from ecology, as Brewer pointed out, that successful systems tend to be those with natural redundancy and resilience.

Operating the Space Station will fundamentally change our understandings of what is feasible and worth doing in space. That is, when we have done experiments on the Station we will find some things more interesting than others. Surely we will find some unanticipated things we want to do. (If we don't it will be, at best, disappointing.) In other words, by definition and by intent we can't tell beforehand what our interests in space will be after we operate the Station. We can only know in advance that they will be different.

But assuming we follow our present track, by the time we learn what is truly interesting we will have spent at least $30 billion and will have a very expensive facility to operate in space. In turn this will generate great pressure to decide that the most interesting activities are the ones that can be done on Station, somewhat analogous to the pressure to put science payloads on Shuttle.[12] Already astronomers are being advised to design observatories that can fly on Station.

Clearly a less risky alternative approach would have been to evolve from Shuttle, to Extended Duration Orbiter, through various Man-Tended Platforms, to a Skylab-type Station, and then to a larger, perhaps permanent Station, learning as we go. In the past, a lack of competition and abundant resources have allowed us to proceed despite our programmatic inefficiency. Neither condition prevails now. How can we take advantage of our strengths to proceed more efficiently? Should we enlarge our criteria of efficiency to encompass more than merely the efficient use of existing or planned space resources?

(8) *Emphasis on operations* may conflict with NASA's charter as an R&D agency. With Shuttle, the great observatories, the Centers, TDRSS, and Station are in place, most of NASA's budget could be devoted to operating infrastructure. Of course the infrastructure supports R&D, but it tends to develop a life of its own, as Waldrop has pointed out. The tendency is for infrastructure operations to increase their share of resources in a ratchet-like manner because they are seldom terminated, and because new programs are difficult to start under severe budget constraints.

The trade-off between R&D and operations can be detrimental

to both. For example, if engineers want to continue to make improvements to Shuttle and this conflicts with launch schedules then both the improvements and the operations might be adversely compromised.

Should the civilian space program be split to have one agency for operations, another for R&D? Splitting the program might give users more freedom in choosing launch vehicles. On the other hand Smith, in this volume, argues for again consolidating all civil space activities in NASA.[13] These are issues meriting research.

(9) *Consideration of alternative* policy and program choices is important. At present most policy and program analysis is done within NASA and with emphasis on technical considerations. The agency has the initiative: Typically other players react to what NASA proposes or does. Although within NASA alternatives may be considered at an early stage, every effort is made to solidify an agency position before a proposal surfaces and is presented to OMB or Congress. For example, alternative approaches to a Space Station were held close and Congress was presented with the approach of building all at once a large, central facility. A measure of the strength of support for NASA programs is the fact that they are largely supported in spite of the take-it-or-leave-it form of presentation.

Other entities, perhaps even commercial ventures, could be enabled and encouraged to introduce competitive alternatives. This is presently resisted by the program culture. Another way to generate alternatives might be to encourage competition between NASA Centers. The idea of making NASA Centers more independent -- somewhat like the DOE national laboratories -- has been raised.[14] Such a step might *allow* intercenter competition. A further step would be to *encourage* competition, not just in proposal-writing but also in results achieved for resources expended.

Such intercenter competition could turn the present organization of the space program into a major asset. The duplication of effort would be justified by an increase in efficiency through competition. In this volume Wheelon has described how competition between Department of Energy labs has helped our national strategic weapons programs. Certainly a basis for the strength of most U.S. science is competition in the peer-review process for project funding, which takes into consideration the previous accomplishments of the principal investigators.

There is a need for research to evaluate these and other ways of generating alternatives. Certainly any proposal to restructure NASA should be carefully explored. Part of the task is to understand more deeply the reason why few alternatives have been generated.

(10) *Policy planning and appraisal* should be emphasized in the space program. Of course there is great emphasis on technical planning of missions, but as discussed above little open consideration of alternatives or strategic planning.[15] Similarly there is a great deal of technical evaluation of hardware, but little program evaluation.[16]

Criticism of programs and policies is not necessarily destructive, even if it appears to threaten a fragile consensus within or outside the space program. A fragile consensus is unlikely to last and, in any case, hiding flaws eventually destroys credibility. Neither the public nor Congress expects perfection unless it is promised -- either explicitly or implicitly through lack of debate. Defensiveness and inflexibility only dissipate political support.

Given the problems discussed above, it seems likely that civilian space policy would be improved if a more vigorous planning and appraisal capability were organized and encouraged within NASA and left open to participation by outside groups. This would provide some redundancy in policy-making, which as Wheelon argues is just as important as redundancy in hardware. How to achieve this is a policy research problem.

BROADENING RESEARCH

We recommend that the foregoing problems of civilian space policy be considered in broader perspective.

Space policy research traditionally has proceeded with little regard for parallel experiences in other areas of policy, or for the various principles of policy inquiry distilled from such experiences. Meanwhile, over the past two or three decades, a new discipline of public policy has begun to emerge from the traditional policy-relevant disciplines.[17] It provides a rich store of practical and theoretical insights into problems of decision and decision process in any area of policy. For space policy, it suggests new observations, new interpretations, and new alternatives that are very much needed in the post-Challenger era, and broader perspectives from which space policy can be reconsidered.

To illustrate what we have in mind, consider rationality as a major theme underlying the ten problems reviewed in the previous section. In the emerging discipline, a rational decision is one that selects the action alternative expected to realize the greatest net benefits. It therefore depends upon the *alternatives* available and upon two kinds of estimates: Estimates of the future *consequences* of each course of action, and estimates of the future *preferences* (or goals) for evaluating those consequences.

Modern theories of rationality recognize, however, that humans are limited; that is, human beings are at best "boundedly rational."[18] For any policy decision, no one can imagine all the possible alternatives, resolve all the uncertainties and ambiguities inherent in the two estimates of the future, and then make an objectively rational decision -- or even come close. Instead, each of us considers carefully only subsets of the possible alternatives, consequences, and preferences, with various degrees of creativity and dependability. And different groups of people tend to consider different subsets in different ways according to the special interests they share. Consequently, in an open and competitive political arena, decisions tend to be controversial and the alternative eventually selected is at best an hypothesis about what is rational.

Improvements in rationality depend upon recognizing this reality and taking advantage of it. More alternatives can be generated if competing interest groups have both the incentive and the ability to take broad and ambiguous goals -- the only goals likely to be widely accepted -- and resolve them into programs that reflect their respective interests. Estimates of future consequences and preferences can be improved through action on multiple alternatives as quasi-experimental trials, conducted in series or in parallel. Decisions can be reconsidered and modified if the commitment to any one alternative is contingent upon the test of experience and limited with respect to the time and resources required to obtain that experience.[19]

In short, since we cannot know in advance what is an objectively rational decision, then we should at least evolve better approximations through procedures that are self-correcting. Such procedural rationality is implicit in the design of the American political system.[20] It is also implicit in the various procedures of modern science, including experimental methods and continuous peer review.

In public policy as in science, the best answers are not handed down from the keepers of a vision. The best answers are those which survive the tests of experience and open debate among informed representatives of different viewpoints. Institutions based on such self-correcting procedures are more rational than any single group participating in them -- provided the participants respect such institutions and allow them to work.

NOTES

1. Both the Apollo and Post-Challenger paradigms are described in the first chapter of this volume. The Apollo Paradigm, briefly, is the set of attitudes and practices, the institutional culture, that developed in the U.S. civil space program largely as a result of the Apollo Program. A core assumption is that large manned space missions are necessary to maintain political support for the civilian space program. The Post-Challenger Paradigm remains to be completely defined but is, or hopes to be, characterized by a more rigorously critical analysis of programs in their actual context.

2. If Shuttle is 98% reliable, the simple probability is 50% that there will be an accident in the next thirty-five flights, i.e. in 1993 before first element launch of Station.

3. Webb, James E., *Space-Age Management: The Large-Scale Approach* (New York: McGraw-Hill, 1969).

4. The Tracking and Data Relay Satellite System was financed by a loan from the Federal Financing Bank which NASA is now paying off, with interest, from its limited budget. See U.S. House of Representatives, Committee on Science and Technology, 98th Congress, *United States Civilian Space Programs, vol. II, Applications Satellites*. Serial M (Washington, D.C.: U.S.G.P.O., May 1983), p. 372 ff.

5. Because funds for government programs are appropriated, costs and cost overruns are treated politically, not economically. Annual spending must fit within the amount appropriated. However, if a project runs into difficulty, the typical response is "stretchout," pushing work into future (appropriation) years, which inevitably raises the total cost of the project in order to hold down the cost in the current year. Most contracts for space projects are (for good reasons) "cost-plus," and lack strong incentives to keep costs down. Finally, the natural tendency for government managers is to ask for *more*, not *less*, money from the appropriations process. See papers by Wheelon and Waldrop, this volume; see also (a) Space Exploration/Cost, Schedule, and Performance of NASA's Galileo Mission to Jupiter, GAO/NSIAD-88-138FS. (b) Space Exploration/NASA's Deep Space Missions are Experiencing Long Delays, GAO/NSIAD-88-128BR. (c)

188

Space Exploration/Cost, Schedule, and Performance of NASA's Magellan Mission to Venus, GAO/NSIAD-88-130FS. (d) Space Exploration/Cost, Schedule, and Performance of NASA's Ulysses Mission to the Sun, GAO/NSIAD-88-129FS. All U.S. General Accounting Office, May, 1988, Washington, D.C. These GAO reports document typical cost overruns by factors of two to three.

6. J. Fletcher, Proceedings of the Fourth National Space Symposium, U.S. Space Foundation, April, 1988, Colorado Springs, CO, p. 160. "To be sure, the Shuttle has done what it was meant to do; it remains the most versatile, flexible, and useful flying machine in the world."

7. This is reflected in their decisions to develop, purchase, and use the Titan IV Complementary Expendable Launch Vehicle (which is approximately equivalent, i.e. complementary, to the Shuttle) and the Delta II and Atlas-Centaur II. See B. Davis, "With its Titan IV, Air Force at Last Takes Helm of Space Program, Putting NASA in the Backseat" *Wall Street Journal*, November 29, 1988, p. A20.

8. Of course this refers primarily to the Challenger accident, but the Rogers Commission report makes it clear that the Shuttle system was breaking down under launch pressure. See Presidential Commission on the Space Shuttle Challenger Accident, *Report to the President*, June 6, 1986, Washington, D.C., Chapter VIII and Appendix J.

9. W. Hively, "A Resurgent NASA Woos Scientists Back to the Space Program," *American Scientist*, March-April, 1989, p. 132.

10. NASA Advisory Council, Space and Earth Science Advisory Committee, *The Crisis in Space and Earth Science* (Washington, D.C.: NASA, November, 1986).

11. Solar System Exploration Committee, NASA Advisory Council, *Planetary Exploration Through Year 2000; A Core Program* (Washington, D.C.: U.S.G.P.O., 1983).

12. This attitude was clear in the agency. For example: "In the coming decade, scientific investigations conducted in earth orbit will be the most important because these take the best advantage of the unique properties of the Shuttle." H. Mark, *The Space Station* (Durham: Duke University Press, 1987), p. 239.

13. A NASA advisory committee is also reported to recommend this approach. See *Defense Daily*, May 26, 1989, p. 321.

14. Committee on Space Policy, National Academy of Sciences, National Academy of Engineering, *Toward a New Era in Space* (Washington, D.C.: National Academy Press, 1988).

15. "Strategic planning is a structured, ongoing process that

systematically identifies an organization's mission and establishes the goals and objectives that need to be achieved to accomplish that mission....strategic planning has not yet been fully implemented throughout the agency....NASA has not yet developed an agency wide strategic plan." From U.S. General Accounting Office, *Civil Space: NASA's Strategic Planning Process*, GAO/NSIAD-89-30BR (Washington, D.C.: November, 1988).

16. There are, however, a few outstanding examples of program evaluation: For example, in reports that followed the Challenger accident; see (a) Chapters VI, VII and VIII of the Rogers Commission report, (see note 8); (b) Chapter II and V of Committee on Science and Technology, U.S. House of Representatives, 99th Congress, *Investigation of the Challenger Accident*, House Report 99-1016 (Washington, D.C.: October 29, 1986), p. 3; "...NASA's drive to achieve a launch schedule of 24 flights per year created pressure throughout the Agency that directly contributed to unsafe launch operations." p. 119; "The Congress and the Executive Branch jointly developed the policy that the Space Shuttle should...provide for most of the Free World's space launch needs. By and large, both Branches failed to appreciate the impact that this policy was having on the operational safety of the system." (c) NASA Advisory Council, *Report of the Task Force on Issues of a Mixed Fleet* (Washington, D.C.: NASA, March 1987). This report recommends that "The Shuttle must be recognized as a national resource of enormous importance to the U.S. space program. NASA policy should evolve from one that has maximized the use of the STS [Shuttle] to a policy that preserves the Shuttle for those missions requiring its unique capabilities." See also *The Crisis in Space and Earth Science* (note 10). This report is in effect an evaluation of our national space and earth science program.

17. See for example, such journals as *Policy Sciences*, the *Journal of Policy Analysis and Management*, and the *Journal of Public Policy*, which represent distinguishable components of the new discipline.

18. See, for example, Herbert A. Simon, *Reason in Public Affairs* (Stanford: Stanford University Press, 1983); and James G. March, "Bounded Rationality, Ambiguity, and the Engineering of Choice," *Bell Journal of Economics* 9 (1978), pp. 587-608.

19. Under a budget constraint, a limited and contingent commitment to any one alternative also increases the feasibility of similar commitments to multiple alternatives.

20. See, for example, Martin Landau, "Redundancy,

Rationality, and the Problems of Duplication and Overlap," *Public Administration Review* 29 (1969), pp. 346-358.

INDEX

ACTS. *See* Advanced
  Communications Technology
  Satellite
Adams, Henry, 35
Adaptation, 168, 177
Advanced Communications
  Technology Satellite (ACTS),
  107, 108, 113-114
Advanced Launch System, 61
Aerospace plane, 61-62, 74, 82(n4)
Agnew, Spiro, 40
Air Force Satellite Tracking
  Facility, 55
Apollo paradigm, 3-5, 6, 39-40,
  122, 141, 156, 175-178,
  187(n1)
Apollo program, 13, 20, 43, 44, 46,
  47, 78, 119-120, 176
Apollo-Soyuz Test Project, 43
Apollo 13, 44
Ariane launch vehicle, 77, 134, 147,
  182
Armstrong, Neil, 36, 40
Astronomy, 65-66. *See also*
  Scientific research
Automated X-Ray Astronomical
  Facility, 27
Automation, 123

Bank of America, 158-159
Becker, Carl, 35
Bell, Alexander Graham, 37

"Block one." *See* Space Station
  program
Brewer, Garry D., 176, 183
Budget. *See* National Aeronautics
  and Space Administration,
  budget
Bush, George, 107, 114

Canada, 31(n14)
Carter, Jimmy, 60, 62, 91, 120, 142
CBS, 158, 159
Centaur upper stage, 90
Centralization, 182-183
Challenger accident, 2, 5, 11, 13,
  18, 19, 22, 34, 46, 52(n51), 58,
  60, 83, 90, 93, 123, 125, 177,
  181, 188(n8)
Commercialization. *See*
  Privatization; Space,
  commercial use of
Communications, 36, 38, 54, 55, 57,
  62, 106-107, 112, 146, 148
Communication Satellite Act
  (1962), 57
Communications Satellite
  (Comsat) Corporation 36, 57,
  114(n3)
Competition. *See*
  Internationalization;
  Privatization
Comsat. *See* Communications
  Satellite Corporation

194

196